V I S U A L

L A N G U A G E

ANYONE who is responsible

for preserving integrity and

consistency in the projection of

their company's personality should

be interested in the visual language

through which it is expressed.

ISUAL

ANGUAGE

ANYONE who is responsible for creating and implementing

a visual identity for a client should be interested in the

visual language through which it is communicated.

SOURCE OF VISUAL STIMULATION – KEEP THEM AS ABSTRACT AS POSSIBLE. *THEY'LL COME IN USEFUL LATER.*

V I S U A L

L A N G U A G E

ANYONE who is fed-up with the tyranny of the 'logo police' should

be interested in visual language as a way of transcending rigid rules.

BODEGAS PALACIO
CASA FUNDADA EN 1894

VISUAL

LANGUAGE

ANYONE who feels that there must be a better way of briefing

designers and avoiding any nasty surprises from their submissions

should be interested in visual language as an objective benchmark.

PLACE THEM SAFELY IN AN ENVELOPE MARKED '**VISUAL LANGUAGE TOOLKIT**'. ADD TO THEM FROM ANY SOURCE OF VISUAL STIMULATION – KEEP THEM AS ABSTRACT AS POSSIBLE. *THEY'LL COME IN USEFUL LATER.*

ANYONE who feels that there must

be a better way of selecting design

than the chairman's personal taste

should be interested in visual language

as an objective benchmark.

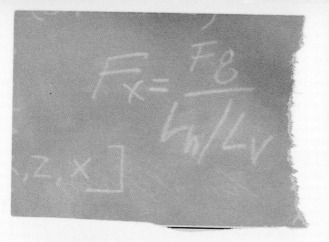

$$F_x = \frac{F_8}{L_n/L_v}$$

$$,z,x]$$

WIN

ET

Susanna takes
step further

with
"You're A Boy,"

album

TRAIL

ε n

ETA

KEEP
BUSH

ST. EMILE

DE

Giò
DE
RGIO ARMANI

THE (PSYCHEDE

Gordon's & Tonic.

1990: TH

Letters of
SILIO FICINO

V I S U A L

L A N G U A G E

ANYONE who cares about meaning as well as form should be interested in visual language as a powerful medium of non-verbal communication.

SOURCE OF VISUAL STIMULATION – KEEP THEM AS ABSTRACT AS POSSIBLE. THEY'LL COME IN USEFUL LATER.

V I S U A L

L A N G U A G E

ANYONE who suspects that more

information is picked up by the 'heart'

than by the 'head' should be interested

in visual language because it has the

power to open the heart.

14 DIJON

All communication takes place through language; not all languages use words...

Visual language

The hidden medium of communication

Client: *"I clearly asked for flowers!"*

You may be using the same word,
but are you speaking the same language?

Designer: *"BUT WE GAVE THEM FLOWERS!"*

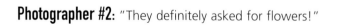
Photographer #2: *"They definitely asked for flowers!"*

Visual

The hidden medium of

language

communication

Peter Bonnici

A RotoVision Book
Published and Distributed by RotoVision SA
Rue Du Bugnon 7
CH-1299 Crans-Près-Céligny
Switzerland

RotoVision SA, Sales & Production Office
Sheridan House, 112/116A Western Road
Hove, East Sussex BN3 1DD, UK

Tel: +44 (0)1273 72 72 68
Fax: +44 (0)1273 72 72 69
e-mail: sales@rotovision.com

Distributed to the trade in the United States by:
Watson-Guptill Publications
1515 Broadway
New York, NY 10036
USA

ISBN: 2-88046-388-2

10 9 8 7 6 5 4 3 2

Book design by Quadrant Design Associates

Production and separations in Singapore by ProVision Pte. Ltd.
Tel: +65 334 7720
Fax: +65 334 7721

Navigating your way through this book

Step 1

Decide if any of the statements on pages 2,4,6,8,10,12 or 14 resonates with you. If they do, detach the first 8 leaves and tear around the images. They're arbitrary shapes, so accurate tearing is not necessary. *NOTE: Tearing is preferable to cutting.*

Pages 1–16

Step 2

Get a sense of the power that non-verbal languages have in the communication process. Compare also body language, and the languages of sound, space, touch, smell...

Pages 24–37

Step 3

Explore the elements of the visual language and see how the elements can come together to create distinctive voices.

Pages 38–77

Step 4

Put visual language in its commercial context of projecting the personality of brands. The role of the logo, style guide, 'visual voice'...

Pages 78–127

Step 5

Explore methods of arriving at the core qualities behind the personality of the brand and how to translate them into the visual language to create a unique 'visual voice' for the brand.

Pages 128–145

Step 6

Explore practical ways of using the 'visual voice' when briefing, creating and evaluating design. *(Here's where you'll find it useful to cut out the inside front flap of this book).*

Pages 146–160 & inside front cover flap

VISUAL LANGUAGE is the 'look and feel' of an item of design — created by such elements as colour, proportion, letterform, shape, texture... It communicates on a level independent of the descriptive elements — literal or symbolic — of the imagery. It conveys emotional messages to its audiences and they 'feel' something about the client, service or product.

It is just one of a range of non-verbal languages with which we are all familiar. We read these languages easily and make judgements based on the messages we pick up through them. Music is the language of sound — it can totally change a person's mood. Related to this is tone of voice — subconscious decisions based on tone of voice sometimes override the meaning of the words being spoken. Then there is body language... and the language of spaces like the impact of an atrium in a building or the feeling of expansion when walking in mountains. Then, of course, there is colour and form and shape and proportion and texture — the basic toolkit of a designer...

*Visual language
is what the
'heart' 'reads'
after the mind
has become
quiet.*

Content of imagery is read
by the intellectual centre.
Visual language speaks to –
and can be 'read' by – the
emotional centre.
No image is devoid of an
emotional message.
Effective communication,
therefore, requires
consistency between content
and mood.

What's going on here?

What's their relationship?

What were her last words?

What's he saying in response?

What's going to happen in ten minute's time?

How do you know?

1 Body language

This is the language of gesture and posture. No words may be exchanged but we know exactly what's being said through this language. It sets off warning bells. There may be cultural differences related to some aspects of body language, but broadly speaking we draw conclusions from it.

Body language shares some common features with visual language because sight is involved. A lot of socio-cultural influences are also at work.

1

2

Is the person in picture #1 ❑ happy ❑ sad ❑ agitated ❑ calm ❑ aggressive?
Is the person in picture #2 ❑ happy ❑ sad ❑ agitated ❑ calm ❑ aggressive?

The expression of the person in picture #2 is more enigmatic than that in picture #1. We might be able to eliminate the extremities of the scale (eg. aggressive), but require more subtle descriptors like 'wistful', 'melancholy', 'dreamy' to describe the state.

The important point here is NOT that there are right or wrong answers, but that we are prepared to describe a state just from body language — the language of the body — without any verbal information.

1 Body language

See note
below

This is the language of gesture and posture. No words may be exchanged but we know exactly what's being said through this language. It sets off warning bells. There may be cultural differences related to some aspects of body language, but broadly speaking we draw conclusions from it.

NOTE **YES** you have read the words on this page before (if you started from the front of the book) — the only difference is the typographic arrangement of the main text, the addition of this note and the colour (ie. a few of the elements of the visual language). The point to observe is how the idea is being received on this reading. Is it easier to concentrate on the images? Less easy? What's the emotional change? Is it more serious? Less serious? If there has been a change noted, then you will have had a small taste of the importance of visual language.

Body language shares some common features with visual language because sight is involved. A lot of socio-cultural influences are also at work.

1   2

Is the person in picture #1 ❑ happy ❑ sad ❑ agitated ❑ calm ❑ aggressive?
Is the person in picture #2 ❑ happy ❑ sad ❑ agitated ❑ calm ❑ aggressive?

The expression of the person in picture #2 is more enigmatic than that in picture #1. We might be able to eliminate the extremities of the scale (eg. aggressive), but require more subtle descriptors like 'wistful', 'melancholy', 'dreamy' to describe the state.

The important point here is NOT that there are right or wrong answers, but that we are prepared to describe a state just from body language — the language of the body — without any verbal information.

2 Sound

SOUND is a very powerful non-verbal language that we are highly adept at 'reading'. In fact we are so adept at reading tone, that we are barely conscious of how frequently we use this powerful faculty of ours.

Communicators in advertising or film are very aware of the role of music in creating emotional responses. The bright, bubbly, feel-good music of The Spice Girls or Abba (whether you like it or not) will be appropriate for creating one mood and the languid music of, say, Debussy will create another.

Music is the language of sound – it can totally change a person's mood. It is such a powerful influencer of mood largely because it relies on the finest of our senses – listening.

In some philosophical systems, music and proportion are closely linked through the mathematics of harmony. Architects are known to have taken the ratios of length, breadth and height of a space and plucked that harmony on a harp. If the sound is harmonious, then they have probably got the relationship right. If not, they look for ways of resolving the discord.

The non verbal languages tend to be linked at a deep level. Images, for example, can be linked to associated sounds.

Look at these two pictures and imagine the music that most accurately reflects each one.

Which one is faster? Which one classical? Which one allows for electronic sounds? What accounts for these qualities visually – over and above the literal information? What is their musical equivalent?

This is how one language is translated into another.

The faculty of translation is an important concept in this book.

The human mind is capable of reading and interpreting messages in non verbal languages subconsciously — and believing them!

People read tone of voice with even more dramatic outcomes.

Try to set aside any judgements based on reading the body language of the people pictured here and try to imagine just their tone of voice.

They are all giving the same answer to the question: **HOW ARE YOU?**

If you have imagined their tone of voice correctly, you will realise how much more you are prepared to believe that tone rather than the actual words they are speaking.

The relation of visual language to design is the equivalent of tone of voice to speech.

Just relying on voice — tone, speed, volume — do you believe some answers and not others? How? Why?

BODY LANGUAGE 55%	VOICE 38%	Content 7%

First impressions take 30 seconds. If we fail to make the right impact only 7% of the message is retained.

Mehrabian, A (1972). Non-verbal communication. Aldine, Chicago.

Sound can also be internal — as when we read. These internal sounds can be just as powerful in shaping the emotional ground.

Now entertain conjecture of a time
When creeping murmur and the poring dark
Fills the wide vessel of the universe.
    From camp to camp, through the foul womb of night,
    The hum of either army stilly sounds,
    That the fix'd sentinels almost receive
    The secret whispers of each other's watch.
Fire answers fire, and through their paley flames
Each battle sees the other's umber'd face;
Steed threatens steed, in high and boastful neighs
Piercing the night's dull ear; and from the tents
The armourers accomplishing the knights
With busy hammers closing rivets up,
Give dreadful note of preparation.
    The country cocks do crow, the clocks do toll,
    And the third hour of drowsy morning name.
Proud of their numbers and secure in soul,
The confident and over-lusty French
The low-rated English play at dice;
And chide the cripple tardy-gaited night
Who like a foul and ugly witch doth limp
So tediously away. The poor condemned English,
Like sacrifices, by their watchful fires
Sit patiently and inly ruminate
The morning's danger; and their gesture sad
Investing lank-lean cheeks and war-worn coats
Presented them unto the gazing moon
So many horrid ghosts.

SHAKESPEARE: HENRY V

On these pages are descriptions of the same battlefield expressed in different tones of voice...

Demoralised and tired British soldiers, without proper equipment, are unconfident as they face a complacent and well-fed French enemy.

It's three o'clock in the morning. You can hear the sounds of horses neighing and the clang of blacksmiths repairing armour. The night sky is pitch black. There is no wind.

The enemy is so close that the British guards can almost hear the secret passwords of their opposite number and see their faces in the light of the campfires.

The French soldiers are drinking and laying bets on how many British soldiers they can kill in the next day's battle. The blood lust is up; the French can hardly wait to finish off their opponents.

The British are dreading the carnage that must surely follow.

Or...

Three a.m. Pitch black night. Eve of battle. Weather conditions fair. Armies in close proximity of one another. Visual and audible contact possible. French forces superior and confident. British forces tired, ill-equipped and demoralised.

The mood created by sentence rhythm, word combination and punctuation produce an effect when sounded aloud to an external listener or even when sounded silently in mind.

QUESTION: Which of the three versions paints the most pessimistic picture of the English chances?
What is it about the Shakespeare version that allows the reader to believe that all is not quite lost? His literal description would lead us to believe that the English are likely to be defeated... but the tone of his language communicates something different...

3 Space

WALK into any space and the emotional impact is obvious.

A huge market has opened for exponents of this non-verbal language – even the most hard-nosed corporations, like banks and major listed companies, are having their offices assessed and turned round by Feng Shui experts.

Non verbal languages:

4 Smell

5 Touch

SMELL is a powerful stimulant of emotion, as supermarkets have known for some time. They find that the smell of fresh-baked bread has a measurable effect on purchase habits.

British Airways pump particular odours into their planes. When this is brought to the attention, most people can remember the experience of the smell, but cannot recall the precise effect it had on them.

Most people, however, can recall
the smell of fresh-cut grass...
of the sea air...
the smell of babies...
furniture wax...
bonfires...
books...
starched sheets...
hotel rooms...
canvas tents...
the first rains...

Smell is closely associated with taste. Hold your nose when eating a banana. It is very difficult to identify the taste, but the moment the nose is released, the taste will come flooding back.

TEXTURE is evocative too.
Shut your eyes and touch a series of objects, from soft feathers to jelly, marble to wood and chrome, pebbles from the seaside and volcanic rock.

The sense of touch does more than inform about what is being touched – it can be reassuring, alerting, comforting or painful.

There is a big difference between eating your breakfast cereal with a metal, plastic or wooden spoon. The mouth is very sensitive to touch – babies explore their new world through it and lovers kiss.

Designers use the sense of touch in choosing materials for brochures – matt or gloss stocks of varying weights, tracing paper dividers and dust jackets, textured papers, matt lamination, UV varnishing, heavy board covers fastened with brass nuts, stickers, embossing, foil blocking....
Multi-layered type and imagery can be seen as a simulation in two dimensions of textures we touch.

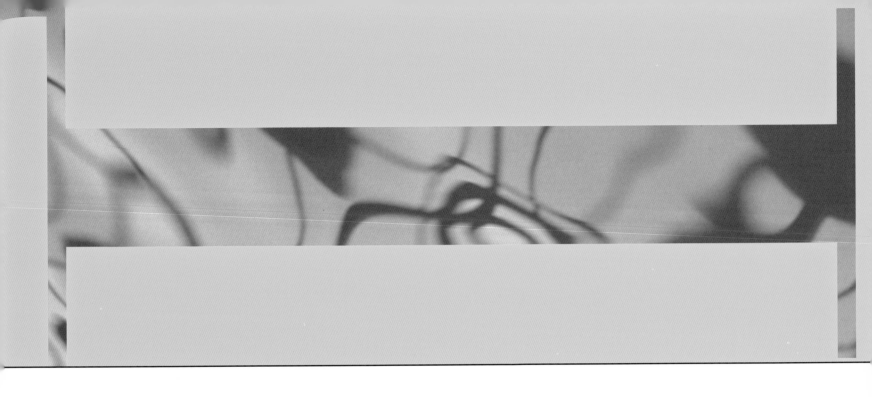

This section introduces the elements associated with the visual language — colour, shape, letterform, proportion, texture and imagery. It ends with a few examples of how the same pieces of information can come together to create different 'visual voices'.

From this point we embark on a journey of discovery.

There are many forces along the way to send the navigator spinning off in one false direction or another. There are underwater rocks to snag the unwary. There are the alluring sirens against whose seductive song the ears will need to be shut tight. There are false dawns and raging storms.

It is essential to find a rudder.

The rudder on this particular exploration will be the emotions – something any communicator in any language wishes to affect. If a message does not move you emotionally – if it does not connect with you deeply – it is unlikely to result in action.

The emotional realm appears to be linked to meaning.

The principal actor in a performance based on a translation of an ancient Sanskrit text could not remember his lines for the final speech. No one could help him by deconstructing the meaning of the text as it was quite difficult to penetrate. The composer working with the production suggested that he wrote some music to accompany the speech. As soon as the music started, the actor's speech flowed and turned out the be the most moving moment of the performance.

The actor's words were not carrying the meaning, nor was his delivery – quite simply he did not understand what he was saying. What carried the meaning was the music! With or without the words, the effect was moving. With the words, the effect was greater than the sum of its parts.

This experience started the author's personal journey. If the language of sound could have such a powerful impact, then what about the language of images – the visual language? Can imagery evoke a feeling of happiness or love – independent of subject matter? Music can!

Once the journey started, there were clues that the visual language had a comparable evocative power – the key is letting that power express itself cleanly. One obstacle is that subject matter is mistakenly taken to be the main strength of the image and the visual language that underpins it is forgotten. Yet, anyone who has stood before the paintings of Mark Rothko or Jackson Pollock will know how moving they are – despite the absence of subject matter.

The chief obstacle, however, appears to be that thinking and feeling have got mixed. People say: I feel this is the right course of action (when they think it) or say: I think that's beautiful (when they feel it)!

Some of the signposts, sirens and underwater rocks passed on the way...

Q: If the *right* and *duty* of a designer is self-expression (as some say), then is the designer's right any more valid than that of the marketing manager's PA who can knock up a leaflet using the standard software on the office computer?

Q: Can so-called 'new visual languages' be judged on the same basis as verbal languages, where usefulness is measured by the vocabulary's ability to express a range of subjects in great depth and communicate through a variety of forms – poetry, fiction, essay, rhetoric, reportage, academe, technical thesis, pun, etc? If they *are* 'new' languages, then are they as useful as English or as limited as Pali when it comes to communicating modern management theory, for example? Or are so-called new languages not languages at all – just the equivalent of, say, Harlem slang to English?

Q: Can the 'either-or' relationship between the creative and the rational be transcended? How can they work together like the two hands of a potter – the inner one expanding and the outer one shaping the form?

Q: Does individuality constitute the heart of design? If not, what does?

Q: Design may be made by the Mac, by the image, by the conscious, or by the subconscious. By the subconscious is best, by the conscious next, next by the image and worst by the Mac. Can the subconscious/ the instinct/ the intuition be valid if no principles of visual language have been studied, or no conscious work on connecting with human nature or the world been undertaken? Why does so much design rest primarily on powerful imagery?

Q: Can commissioners of design really judge the offerings of the designer if they do not understand the visual language? Can they be taught? Can anyone be taught or is the designer the only rare species that understands the visual language?

People may be divided by ideas, but find common ground in feelings.

Every exercise of creating visual benchmarks with a client group (described on Page 134) starts off with the group operating in the habitual 'thinking' mode. Every choice of image by one person is resisted by at least one other – that's when they are judging imagery as information or symbol. At some point in the process one person gets the idea that the exercise is about feelings and not about ideas and they start to operate through feelings. Others feel free to follow. When they are in this 'feeling' mode, the level of disagreement plummets!

Go

Elements of the visual language:

1 colour

COLOUR SPEAKS
It is an element of the visual language and has a meaning on its own

passion and rage

COLOUR SPEAKS
Imagine the effect of living in a room this colour.

peace and calm

COLOUR SPEAKS
Imagine reading a novel printed on paper this colour

traditional and conservative

COLOUR SPEAKS
Have you agreed with the captions to the colours so far?

light and happy

passion and rage

Elements of the visual language:

2 Letterform

LETTER FORM is another aspect of the visual language. We make judgements – like 'modern', 'old fashioned', 'cutting edge', 'bland', 'fun', 'chic'– based simply on letterform.

It is possible to argue that this ability is based on association and context. However, there are qualities intrinsic in the form and shape of lettering that sets up an emotive vibration independent of association.

Research into peoples' response to type has shown that some types make people happy, others make them sad. In one study, the surprise finding was that serif fonts were generally more likely to make people sad than sans serif fonts.

AmoebiaRain

AGaramond

Bauer Bodoni

Bembo

Frutiger

Helvetica

Matrix Inline Script

Shelly Allegro Script

... but also each 'family' of letter forms has variations of weight — shifting from elegance to brashness — and, when combined with colour, multiply the emotive permutations several fold.

Rr

Frutiger Light

Rr

Frutiger Roman

Rr

Frutiger Bold

Rr

Frutiger Black

Rr

Frutiger Ultra Black

Rr

Rr

Rr

Rr

Rr

Rr

If a letter form is seen as a graphic shape rather than a linguistic symbol, then the qualities become even more apparent.

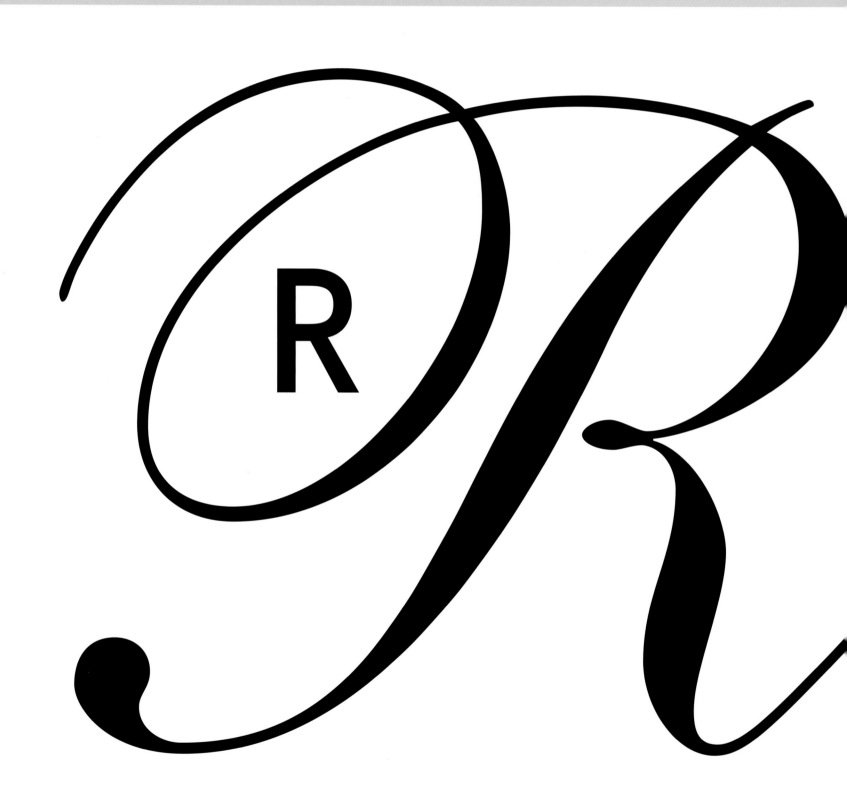

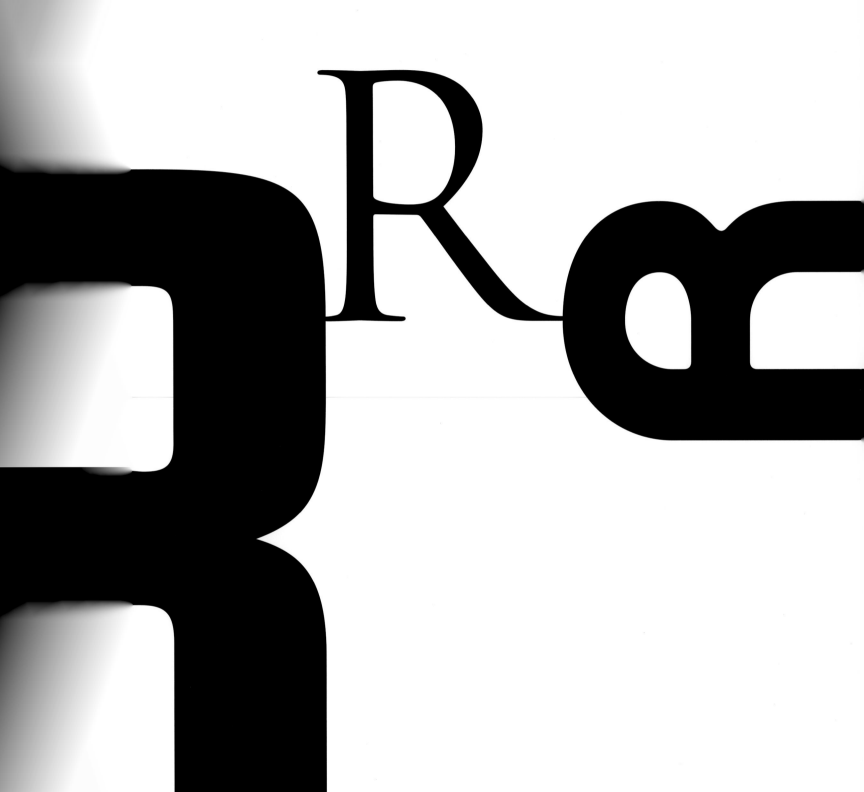

Elements of the visual language:

3 Shape

GRAPHIC SHAPE is one small step away from letter form – a step of abstraction.

These too are part of the visual language palette. These too create emotional shifts. In combination they create patterns. Add colour and there is an enormous range of variations.

Are some shapes more likely to project 'corporate' qualities? Are some more 'community' oriented?

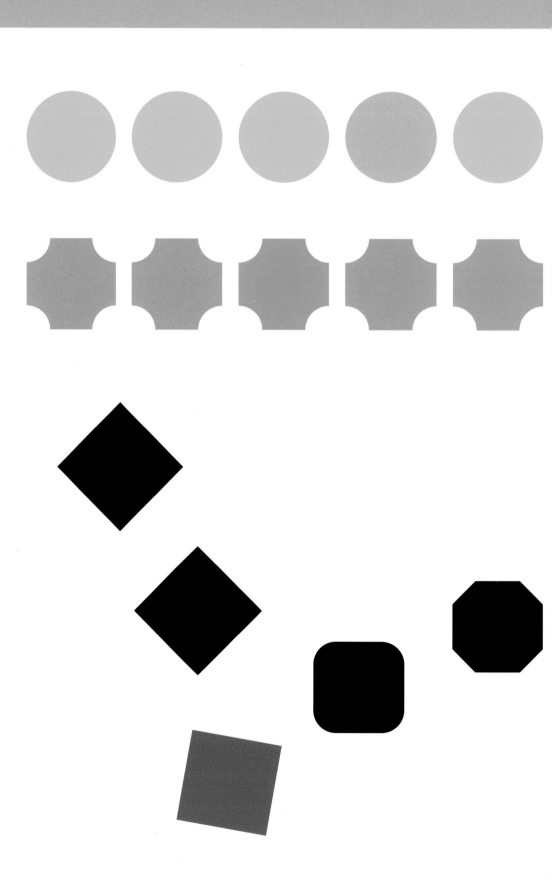

The border on this page is a shape.

Even fine rules
are 'shapes'

what's the
emotional effect
of these shapes?

If these were images in different tour operator brochures:

- Which holiday do you feel would be the most conventional? • Which one is going to be lively and fun?
- Which one is the most expensive? • On which one would you meet smart, trendy people? • Which do you trust?

There aren't obvious answers. Don't try to second-guess the author's intention.

Don't try to rationalise your response — stop analysing — just note the emotional effect.

Cover the pictures so that you view them one at a time and are not treating this spread as a whole. Does your opinion change?

Imagine that the whole brochure uses only one shape of picture —
all images are either eccentrically cropped, or cropped into an organic shape or circle or square.

It's important to note that you would be prepared to make a judgement based on shape.
It is not important to know the 'right' answer — because there is no right answer.

Does this background colour make you change your opinion? Now...
- Which holiday do you feel would be the most conventional? • Which one is going to be lively and fun?
- Which one is the most expensive? • On which one would you meet smart, trendy people? • Which do you trust?

Don't try to rationalise your response — stop analysing — just note the emotional effect.

PROPORTION AND SPACE is another aspect of the visual language. It affects the reception of information. This has been a principle of aesthetics with a long history — from the golden ratio to other harmonic proportions.

Look at each of the squares below – ONE AT A TIME – and note the different feelings created by the space taken up by the image. You will feel comfortable with some and not so comfortable with others...

a

b

d

Not only are different impressions created by size and shape in a given space, but also by position in that space. You might find that the 'message' of a particular shape in a particular position could be at odds with the 'message' given out by colour. Whilst there is conflict, the viewer feels that 'it doesn't quite work'. When the visual messages of the conflicting elements are re-aligned, we think 'it works'. Consistency is key to ease of communication.

Whilst the size and position of the images in *(e)* and *(f)* 'work' fairly well, the shape and position of *(g)* doesn't work as well. A change of background colour *(h)* appears to make a difference... (This is explored further on the next pages).

e

f

g

Which of these combinations 'work'? In this context, 'work' means feeling an instant YES – without having to think about it. If you find that you can think of a reason why you think it works (e.g., 'The background colour picks up a theme from within the picture,') then you are probably missing the point.

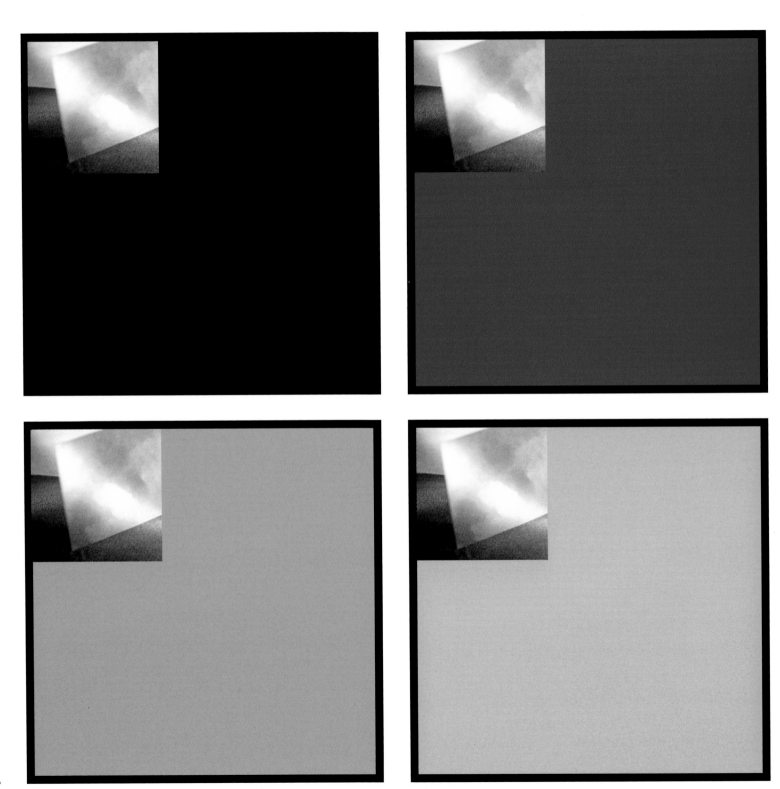

THE MESSAGES OF THE VISUAL LANGUAGE ARE NOT ACCOMPANIED BY ANY REASON OR JUSTIFICATION – THEY ARE TOTALLY INSTINCTIVE. (The only possible explanation of why some work and others do not would be that the various 'visual voices' are harmonious or otherwise).

It will certainly help if you make the effort to cover all the others when assessing each combination.

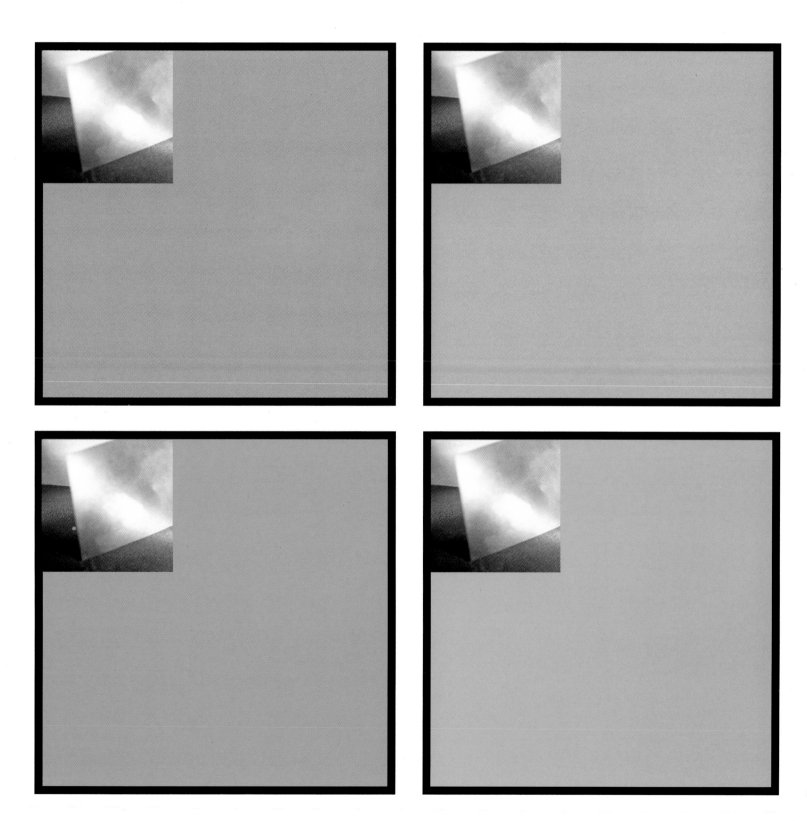

NOW which of these combination 'work'?

If some that didn't work as strongly on the previous spread start to work better now, then it indicates that POSITION is a valid component of visual language.

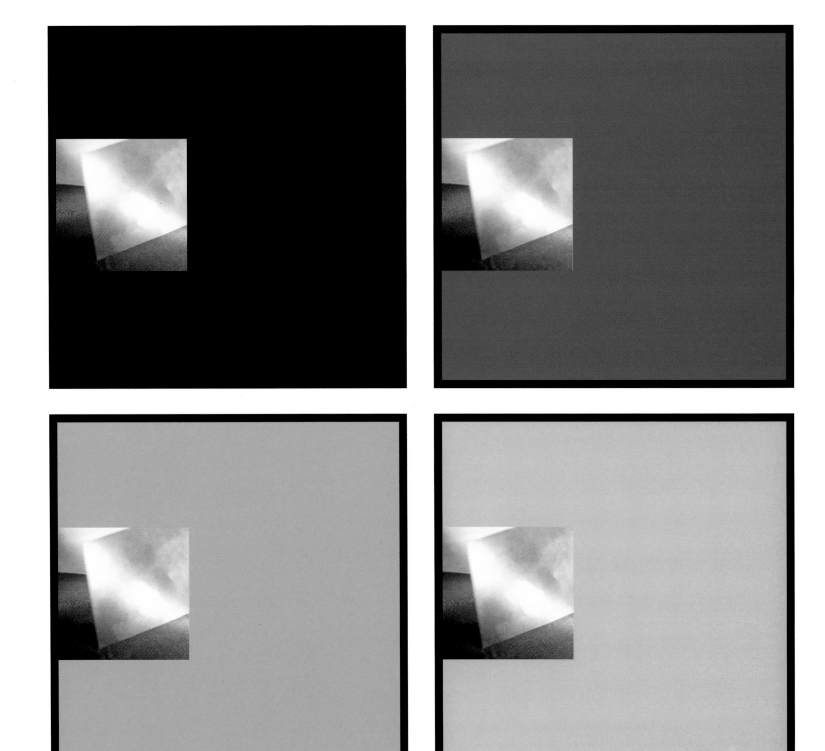

The message conveyed by colour and the message conveyed by position can either reinforce one another or can contradict one another. Remove the conflict and we say: it works.

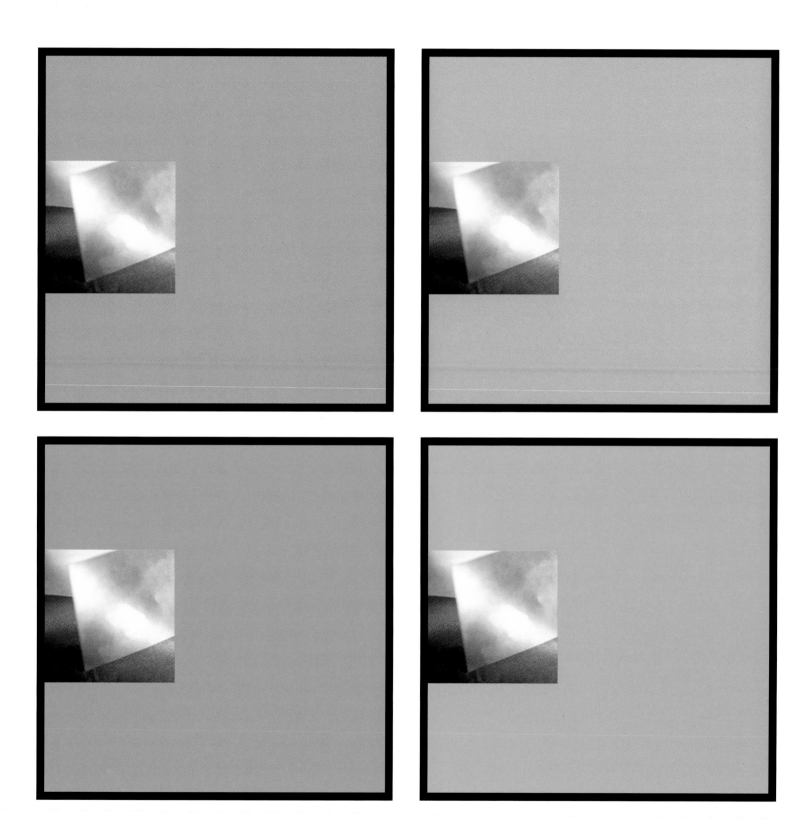

5 Tone and texture

TONE AND TEXTURE create different moods. These could take the form of illustration, photography or digital manipulation.

They include such factors as blur, focus, mark-making, accidental distortions, etc.

The images on this page are all abstract to avoid the distraction/confusion that arises when the subject of the image can be read.

Visual language is <u>not</u> dependent on the subject of the image.

The panel above uses tone in a crude – yet unfortunately common – way. (Computers have a lot to answer for!)

Textures and tones are now so common a feature in design that big business is made in the copyright-free CD business selling images like the ones above.

The layout of this spread, employing as it does a variety of non-harmonious textures, requires great perseverance from the reader. It shows that, even at this level, consistency of language is important for ease of communication.

OF COURSE TONE AND TEXTURE ARE THE CHARACTERISTICS OF CERTAIN TYPEFACE AND CAN BE CREATED BY TYPE SIZE, LEADING, TRACKING, ETC. THERE IS ALSO THE MATTER OF THE TEXTURE OF PAPERS — WHICH ALTHOUGH IT HAS A VISUAL ELEMENT, STRICTLY BELONGS TO THE LANGUAGE OF TOUCH.

The use of tracing paper, heavy embossed boards, metallic papers and inks, die-stamping, laminating, labels... are all part of the visual language (as well as the language of touch).

Added to the list will need to be BINDING. Perfect binding, wiro binding, bindings with brass screws, rivets, staples, thread sewn. All these have to be seen to realise the emotional effect they have on their audiences.

Images, strictly speaking, are not elements of the visual language as we have been using the term in this book.

They are fully-formed expressions that use elements of the visual language such as colour, proportion, tone, texture, etc.

In this sense, they can be termed 'visual voices'.

IMAGES in the form of photographs or illustrations are what most people mistakenly take visual language to be.

These are obviously expressions that use the visual language, but their primary function is to convey information.

Taking speech as a parallel, we have all had the experience that it sometimes happens that the tone of voice (the visual language) conveys a message that contradicts the words being spoken (the descriptive content of the image).

Where the balance is struck between content and style – or information and evocation – is what makes the difference between one image and another – even though the subject may be the same (see images below).

Context matters

Where one strikes the balance – a greater emphasis on description vs a heavier leaning towards evocation – will be determined by context.

If you were publishing a book on botany, for example, you would want the pictures of flowers to be as descriptive as possible without any distracting distortions that stylists impose. If you were trying to evoke a feeling of the peace and beauty of nature, the overall mood of the imagery would dominate over the description.

There is another distinction, however, that is very important. An image can be descriptive on two broad levels: literal or symbolic. This would also determine the visual voice used.

Client: *"I clearly asked for flowers!"*

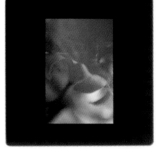

Literal or symbolic descriptions

Sticking with the image of a flower... On a literal level we might recognise that the flower is a rose, for example. The rose, however, also happens to have become the symbol of a number of Social Democratic Political Parties in Europe.

If the rose is used in this symbolic way, then it can also be assigned the burden of evoking the values that Social Democratic Parties espouse – liberty, equality, fraternity.

The rose as a symbol of liberty will need to be represented in a way that evokes the feeling of freedom – with qualities such as openness, energy, excitement, potentiality... *(Quite different from a rose in a botany book!).*

Also, on a more general level, flowers could be used as symbols of 'growth' or 'freshness', 'sophistication' or as reminders that 'beauty fades'. Each of these roles would shift the balance more towards the 'evocation/style' end of the spectrum and the literal description takes second place.

It is important, therefore, for image-maker, designer and client commissioner to be aware of what's really being asked for at the briefing stages. The client could ask for flowers imagining a more literal description. The designer could want to convey, through the use of art photography, that the client has style or street cred. The photographer, on the other hand, might have a point of view which is different from either of the two above.

Photographer #2:
"They definitely asked for flowers!"

There are no right or wrong images. There are just appropriate or inappropriate visual voices.

Designer: "BUT WE GAVE THEM FLOWERS!"

Let's put it all together...

Using the same information content and the range of visual language elements to speak in different visual voices...

Here are 4 components of content:

1
A photographic image

2
A statement

"Imagination is the highest kite you can fly."

3
A graphic image

4
Page dimension

240

290

Pages 73-75 are the designer's presentations of your job. You are a sharp, innovative and well-managed company communicating to other companies like yourself. Which layout reflects your qualities?

i MAGINATION

IS THE HIGHEST KITE

YOU CAN FLY.

IMAGI NATION

74

is the highest kite you can fly.

Imag
ination
is
the h igh es τ
kite

you can fly

Summary so far

1. **Visual language** is the 'look and feel' of an item of design that communicates independently of the descriptive content (literal or symbolic) of text and images.

2. Visual language has its parallels — namely other languages that communicate without the use of words. We are accustomed to reading these languages — sometimes on a very subtle level. Examples are the language of sound — music, tone of voice, rhythm in sentence construction — and the language of posture, expression and movement — body language. And smell. And taste. And touch. And the sense of space.

3. Visual language has a number of basic elements: colour, letterform, graphical shapes, proportion, tone and texture, and imagery. Each of these independently alters the emotional state. In combination, however, their own independent messages may be altered.

Tentative conclusion:

Visual language isn't about a simple one-to-one relationship between visual element and message. In combination, the various elements can either magnify their individual qualities or conflict (creating a nagging feeling of unease). And... this is before we take into account the literal and symbolic meanings in imagery.

So what?

Any organisation wishing to communicate through a visual medium needs to realise that, irrespective of the words they use, independent of the descriptive content of the pictures used to illustrate their message, the **visual language** in which the words and images are clothed is projecting a message of its own. It projects **qualities** such as freshness, modernity, stability, responsiveness, care, dependability, flexibility, incisiveness, intelligence... **And the audience subconsciously 'reads' these messages which can sometimes override explicit messages in text and images.** Thus, an organisation wishing to communicate that 'care' is one of their core qualities might use an image of mother and child. But an indifferent typography and a dull colour and a mediocre crop might all subconsciously communicate a message of carelessness and lack of attention to detail or quality. The image and words might describe 'care', but the visual language evokes 'careless'. And, as we tend to trust our reading of tone of voice rather than words spoken, similarly, the message of the visual language may be the dominant one.

That's what!

Visual language in context

A working understanding of visual language — both by designers and commissioners of design — will eliminate mixed messages and strengthen the communication.

This section places visual language in its commercial context as a medium through which the personality of 'the brand' is communicated. It explores its relation to visual identity, the logo and visual voice and looks at approaches to achieving consistency.

For designers, the value of intuition, instinct and accident is very important — through these routes emotional effects are produced, new forms are created, strong images are devised. Catching the attention in a field which is dominated by screaming images appears to be the over-riding task.

From the point of view of visual language, however, the questions become:

Having caught the attention, what are we really saying?

What emotional messages are we evoking?

What is the effect on the viewer?

A description of the intuitive design process at work.

David Carson: 2nd sight.
Text by Lewis Blackwell

"...The positioning of the title and its imagery is explored by experimentation, each stage spurring the thinking for the next, rather than an initial concept being worked towards. The title, dateline and body copy become increasingly unified, while still carrying the hierarchy of the messages. The piece gains power as the white space emerges to take over more than half the poster, and the accidental arrival at a strange peak in the middle left (created by the cropping of an image) suggests another link with the mountain setting of Aspen, at the same time as creating a diagonal line with the star (itself an image picked out of an archive of experimental, rejected, found, photographed and supplied images collected by Carson)."

On an aesthetic level, the strength of the final piece is obvious. The use of a 'signature' designer may be enough of a message for those who read the poster as a symbol. It will say something like: Carson is cutting edge, so Aspen is cutting edge.

From the point of view of visual language, try the following: Set aside the knowledge that Carson is the designer, and imagine that these are posters for 4 competing design conferences... Which of the conferences do you expect to be the most stimulating? From which one will you expect to learn something of pragmatic use? Which one has speakers who are able to communicate their messages clearly and articulately? In which one will will the speakers be more intellectual and introspective? **All around the world, marketing managers need answers to these sorts of questions in the course of their day-to-day businesses in order to attain and sustain a competitive edge.**

An appreciation of the power of visual language is essential for marketeers whose responsibility is to communicate corporate values. For them it is crucial to differentiate between the marketing message and the brand personality. The former is communicated through ideas, words, images and symbols; the latter through a consistent visual voice that translates and evokes the essential qualities of the brand.

Getting some fuzzy terms straight...

The term 'brand' is fast becoming today's synonym for good old fashioned 'corporate identity'. Today we speak of brand values, brand identity, brand personality, whereas yesterday's talk was of corporate values, corporate identity, corporate image. Yesterday 'brand' referred to commodities, today it relates to the corporation as well.

This book uses the term 'brand' for corporate identity when it is employed **as an essential feature** in communicating and marketing the company's products and services.

Before today's technological and information revolution – called by some 'The Third Industrial Revolution' – product was king. In the Third Industrial Revolution, products have become homogenised. It is difficult to build sufficient market share with a new invention today because analytical and manufacturing technology is so sophisticated that the competition will soon catch up. Differentiation and competitive edge is achieved by bundling together products with services.

Here's where the corporation's personality and values are called upon to add perceived value to 'me-too' products. <u>Example:</u> The perceived qualities of a company like Richard Branson's Virgin are lent to an entertainment chain, an airline, a rail franchise, financial products, cola and condoms. When used in this way, **Virgin is a corporate brand**.

The logo is the most succinct visual expression of a company's identity.

Important judgements are made, based simply on reading the visual language of the logo.

You are searching for a joint-venture academic partner for a piece of ground-breaking research.

All the universities you contacted seemed to have the right technical qualifications, could meet the budget and timescale.

You are a young, innovative, forward-looking company.

Which of these universities do you feel you'd be comfortable working with? You can shortlist just three.

1

2

3

4

5

6

7

8

9

10

11

12

13

14

15

16

Companies will invest a lot of time and money to create a unique visual identity. Their corporate marque becomes a badge on products, signage, stationery, advertising, sales literature, etc. If, however, they do not pay similar attention to creating a unique visual voice which is consistent with the 'voice' of their logo, their original investment will not be working as hard as it could.

A

B

C

G

H

I

THE GENERAL 'VOICE' TEST

On this spread we have the corporate marques of 12 top international or global companies. Each has its own unique qualities.

Step One: Study them individually and connect with their qualities.

Step Two: Match them to the pages from their Annual Reports overleaf.

(this might be easier if you photocopy these pages)

D

E

F

J

K

L

1

2

5

6

9

10

A–2; B-9; C-3; D-5; E-7; F-4; G-6, H-11; I-8; J-12; K-1; L-10.

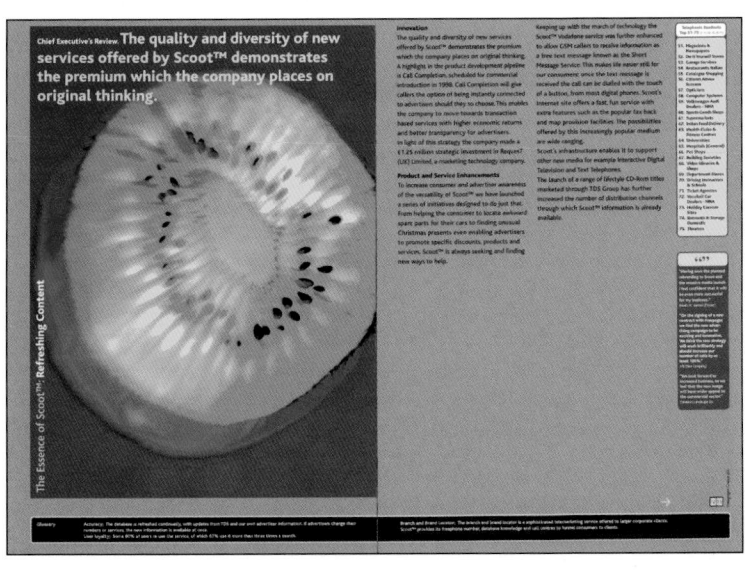

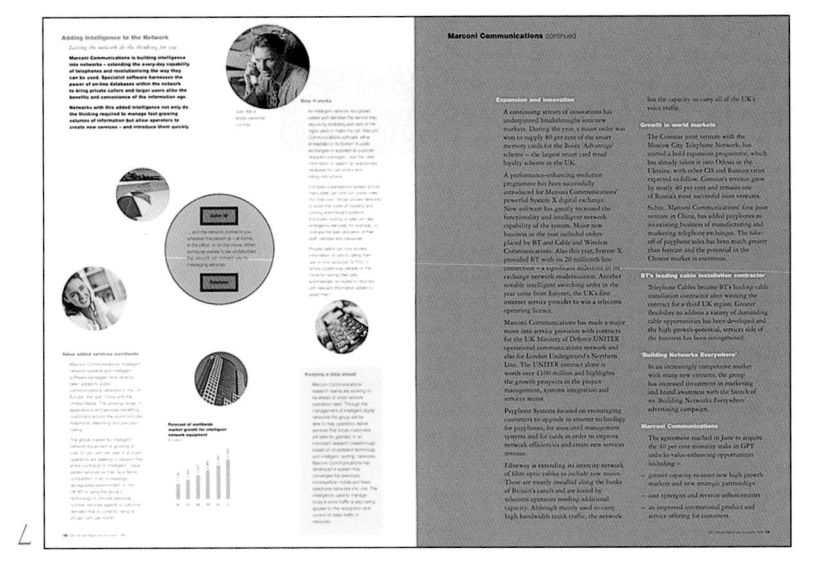

the text and pictures. To help this process, we have printed the spreads upside down.

Mixed messages confuse

The previous test shows that, while logos may be unique in look and feel, their qualities are not necessarily reflected in the pages of Annual Reports — the flagship document of a company.

The visual voice of the logo and the visual voice of the pages are not necessarily communicating the same message. Uniqueness is lost.

Sometimes, this mixed message starts right on the cover...

On the pages that follow we show the covers of Annual Reports. The objective is to test whether the look and feel created by the imagery, typography and layout are projecting the same message as the logo.

Step one: Allow the eyes to rest on each cover so that you can connect with its qualities...

Step two: Cover up the logo and note if
a] the overall feel improves
b] it feels as if something is lost
c] there is no change

ANALYSIS: If [a], then the logo and imagery may be projecting different messages.
If [b], then the qualities of the logo are being magnified by the imagery.
If [c], then the logo and imagery are projecting identical messages.

Annual report and accounts 1998

BT

MATERIALS TECHNOLOGY

AVIATION

Building global businesses through investment and technology

ANNUAL REPORT & ACCOUNTS 1997

Druid Group PLC Annual Report & Accounts
Year ended 30 June 1998

DRUID®

Annual report and accounts 1997

GRANADA

GRANADA GROUP PLC

LASMO

**Annual Review and
Financial Summary**
1997

The mixed message story does not end even if the cover test has been broadly successful [as in the case of BAA and the Riverside Mental Health Trust shown here].

Next comes the page turning test for mixed messages.

The question to ask is: 'Am I in the same brochure?'

Having absorbed the qualities projected by the cover, do you expect what you see as you turn the pages? Are readers' expectations reinforced or undermined?

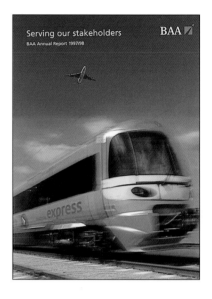

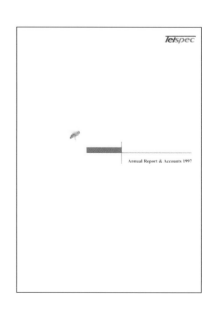

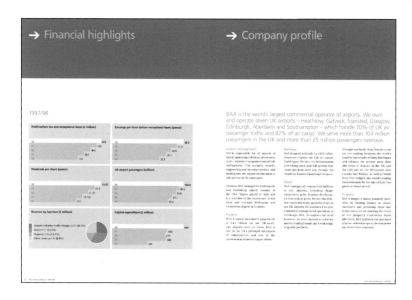

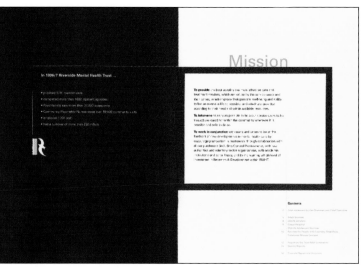

Consideration of visual voice can be broadened to include various media. Mixed messages across media could cause confusion [see opposite page]. A consistent voice will reinforce the message.

At all times, it needs to be remembered that non-verbal languages communicate messages through the medium of feelings.

The matter of consistency can then be deepened by asking if body language, the language of space, the language of tone of voice are projecting the same "feel" as the visual language.

Q: Which of these pubs called 'The George Inn' is among the oldest in London?

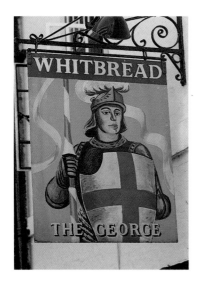

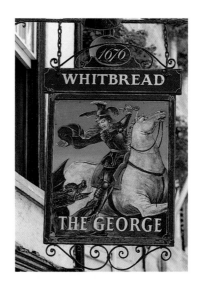

A: All of them — they're the same pub!

So what? Isn't good design what it's all about? Surely it's the idea that counts. Great images, inventive type, pushing boundaries... this is what really counts.

Great images, inventive type, pushing boundaries... this does count. It's like adding words, phrases and idioms to a language. During his working life, Shakespeare added more new words, phrases and idioms to the English language than has been added by all writers in the 400 years since. The English language is richer for him.

In addition to this great gift, however, Shakespeare's plays speak profoundly to the heart, they evoke a variety of emotions and convey multi-layered messages. He wasn't just a linguistic technician.

With computer technology, designers can add a huge amount to the visual vocabulary. Some may have mastered the tools of the trade. But mastery of skills and tools is only the first step of three...

In a delightful book by Gu Gan, '*The Three Steps of Modern Calligraphy*', the author describes **Knowledge of Skills** as: how to use the brush, how to use the ink, the structure of the Chinese characters, composition – a step of intellectual thinking. The second step, **The Link-up with all Matters**, is the link-up with the artistry of calligraphy, the link-up of calligraphy with other arts, connecting with Human Beings and the Great Nature – a step where feelings are cast into the work. The third step is **The Grasp of Essence**. It's a step of inspiration that gives a soul to the bones and flesh of the first two steps. It's a step into freedom.

The ideas in this book address the design equivalent of just the second step – a link up with the feelings behind form. That's what.

"Solutions..."

Various strategies are adopted to eliminate confused messages.

Corporate colours, typefaces, layout grid and cover formulae are meticulously laid down in the corporate identity manual. This is the most common approach.

The formulae can either be rigid or could leave an area of discretion for the designer to innovate. The big fear is that, if the loopholes are too wide, the designer's need to innovate will undermine the intention.

Every designer must know the effect of being jumped on by the 'logo police' and the 'style manual mafia'. The majority of these people stick to the letter of the law and miss its spirit. They mainly tackle the question of <u>visual conformity</u> and do not realise that <u>visual consistency</u> is the true goal.

Their focus is mainly at the first level – 'Knowledge of Skills' – addressed at colour and composition.

Without an appreciation of visual language, however, even the most ardent style police will not notice how inconsistent the messages can become – despite the conformity of style.

Conformity is achieved by rules. Consistency is a matter of voice. Balance is the key.

the formula...

the manual

The corporate identity manual is the rulebook of standards...

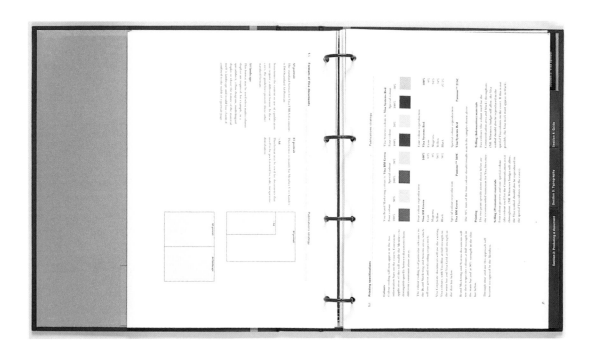

It contains typeface, colour, grids, formats, samples... etc, etc, etc

A simple grid based on halves, quarters, eights, etc.

Type: Bembo and Frutiger families

What the corporate designer had in mind...

Sticking to the letter of the law while taking the first steps to losing the fresh feel and balance...

This internal client wanted more punch and movement. And didn't like 'nursery colours'.

Type: Bembo and Frutiger families...

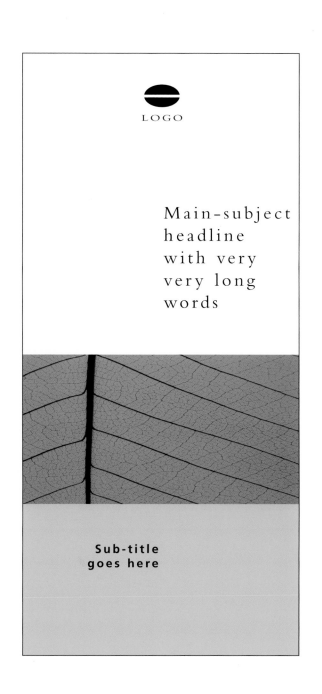

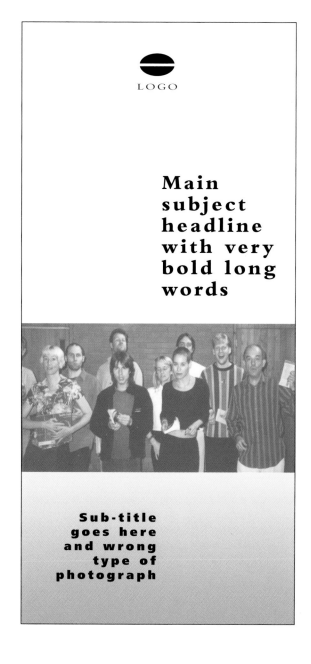

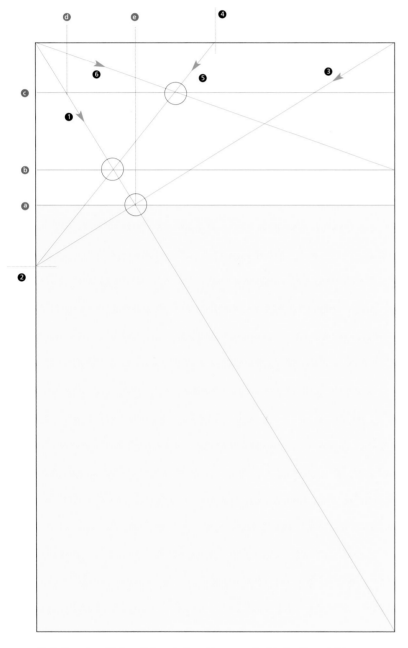

Early Penguin grid: Overall shape is the golden rectangle. 1 is the diagonal; 2 is a square from the bottom; 3 is projected next to cut the diagonal and give us [a] the picture line; 4 is half the width; 5 is projected from it to cut the diagonal and give us [b] the bottom of the title space and thus the point to which project 6; the intersection of 5 and 6 gives [c] the top of the title space, [d] the logo space and [e] the title starting point.

This grid (and minor variations of it) served Penguin and Pelican well until the mid-60s. One could recognise the range of books simply by reading the style, and the brand was associated with quality to such an extent that the reader felt reassured even if they did not recognise the author or the title. (The example above shows the first step of variation).

Abandoning the formula can destroy the brand identity (and maybe the brand itself).

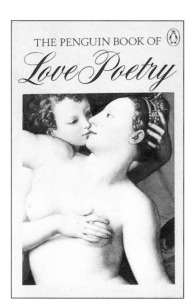

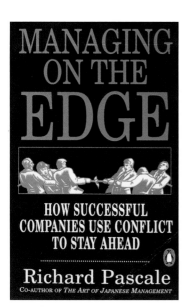

Today it is difficult to recognise a Penguin book from the mass of others. With the abandonment of its visual language, the company lost its unique brand and the associated qualities that have been built up over the years.

The formula can be set as far back as the letterhead. In this example, the ratios A:B, A1:B1, A2:B2 are the Golden Ratio of the Fibonacci series. The yellow rectangle is the Golden Rectangle.

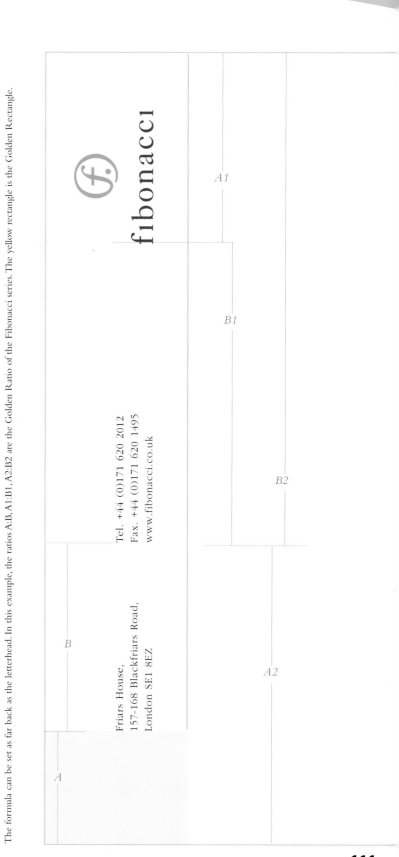

The illustrations on these pages are inspired by Kandinsky's 'Points, Lines and Planes'.

A. Diagonals and halves.

B. Same positions, same angles, varied lengths.

C. Diagonals in same position, same angles, varied lengths.

D. Diagonal angles, lengths and position varied and repeated, vertical and horizontal angles the same, lengths and positions vary.

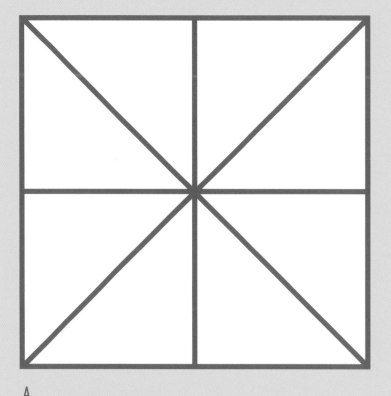

A

C

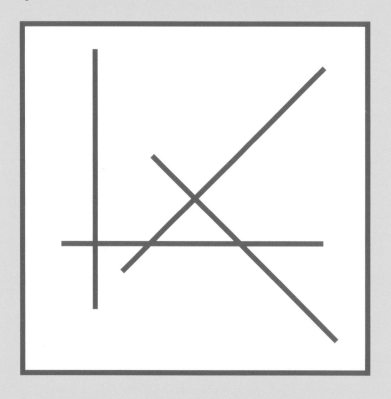

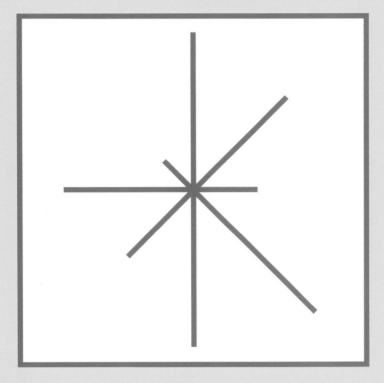

B

D

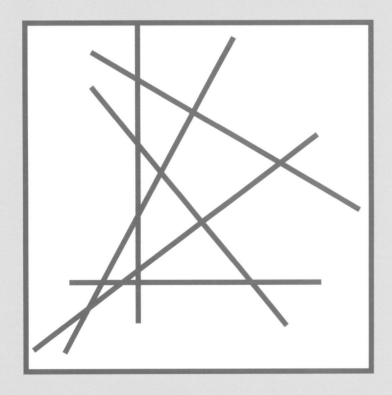

Connect with the underlying steadiness of A and B; the sheer power of disciplined energy in B; the relative balance, combined with energy of C; and the dynamic freedom of D.

Note how eye, mind and heart are steady when looking at A and B, relatively steady when looking at C and move around with D.

Visual language is about evoking qualities like steadiness, disciplined power, energy, freedom, dynamism...

The movements of eye, mind and heart give us the clue to what is happening.

Imagine a style manual that told designers that the effect they were after was closest to A.

Is this workable?

See over....

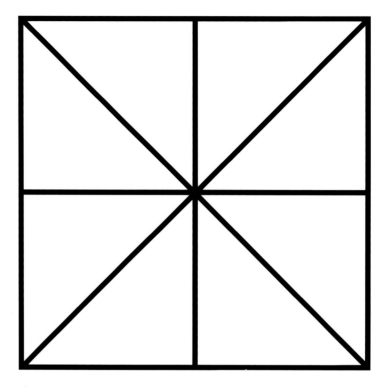

A

C

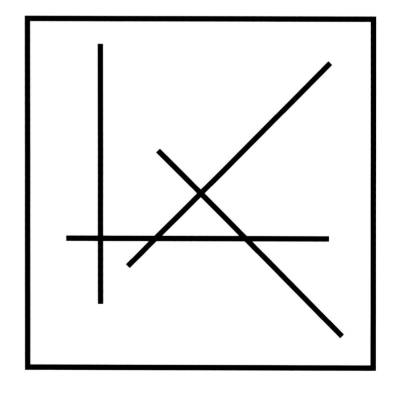

Assessment: Does the eye take in the above layout in one glance — i.e., is it content to rest wherever it falls? Or does it move around the space? If it moves, how much does it move?

114

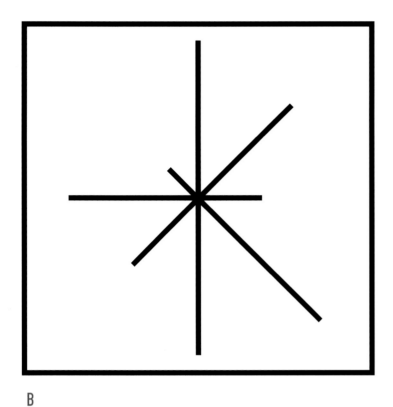

B

D

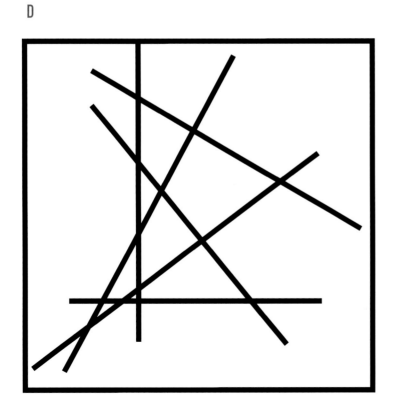

Assessment: Does the eye take in the above layout in one glance – i.e., is it content to rest wherever it falls? Or does it move around the space? If it moves, how much does it move?

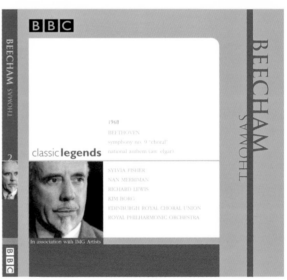

Most restricted: The designer can only choose the background colour (and even then from a restricted pallet to keep in style).

Rigid: The designer can choose pictures and secondary colours.

Which visual voice says 'exclusive' or 'mid-range' or 'collectable' or 'good value'?

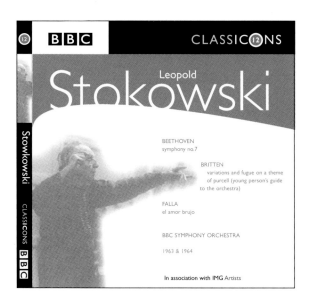

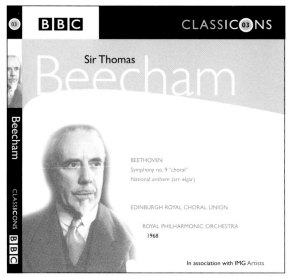

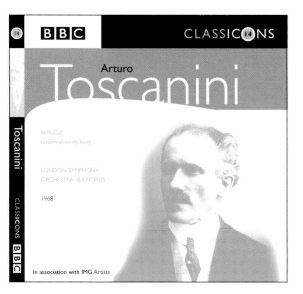

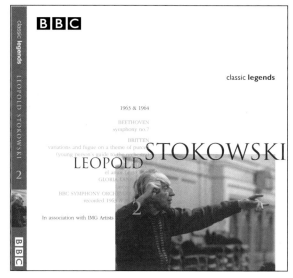

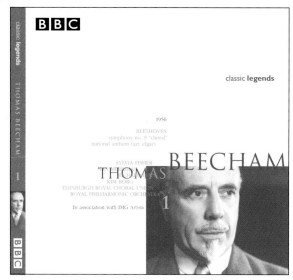

Balanced: Colour, picture and typographic variations possible without loss of identity.

Flexible: visual voice determines the variations – all elements (except typeface and logo position) vary without changing visual voice.

 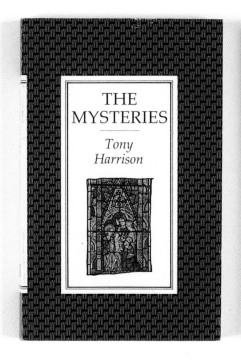 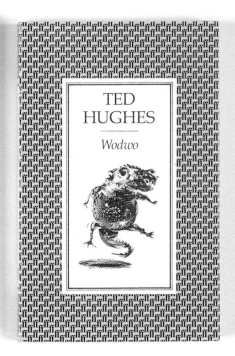

The Faber books (above) allow for variations of imagery and colour, but recognition relies primarily on the strength of the border style.

The Dorling Kindersley books (right) do not even have a 'corporate' typeface or fixed position for the logo. Yet the look and feel of these books is instantly recognisable from across a bookshop. This is an example of the 'visual language approach' to consistent brand image.

Competitors producing a variation of the Faber formula will not necessarily be accused of plagiarism, *but those who copy the DK formula might be!* This is an example of the protection that a unique visual voice can give.

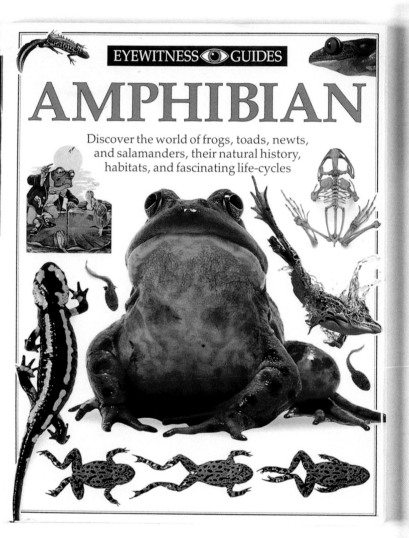

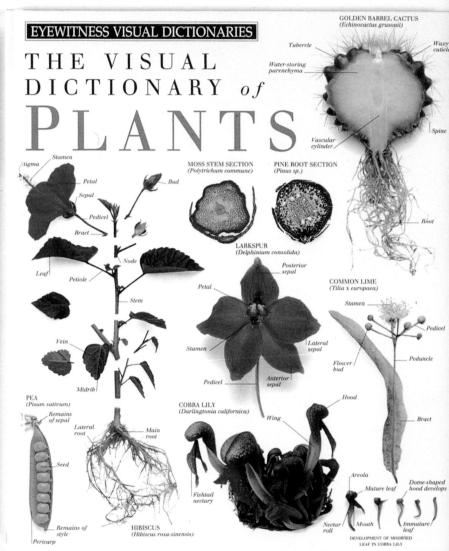

It is interesting to note how much more variation there was in the earlier issues of *Face* – when the designer was still very hands-on, innovating and working from instinct within the given parameters.

RayGun was unique in abandoning even the notion of a fixed masthead...

The questions raised by this 'visual language' approach are: How dependent is it on the individual designer's sensibilities and vision? Is it bound to become a mechanical formula in time? To what extent can the emotional aspect of the look and feel – rather than just the surface level of 'use of skills' – be passed on?

The grid imposed on this A4 page involves halving the space into meaningful sized units.

The various elements of the composition fit in with this grid as follows:

- The logo is $\frac{1}{4}$ width

- The brackets take up
  $\frac{3}{4}$ width
  or $\frac{1}{2}$ the width
  or diminish in units of the grid
  If going up to to the dotted blue line, enlarge logo to 3 units wide.

- Title type sits in brackets.

- The image areas shown in yellow are of two types:
  A: should be fully used i.e., filled with a picture,
  or partially filled with a picture and 'topped up' with a tint,
  or filled with a tint panel on which type is over-printed

  B: height and width can vary, but never wider than orange bracket and never deeper than base line of bottom bracket.

  IMAGES can also fit in cross-hatched areas

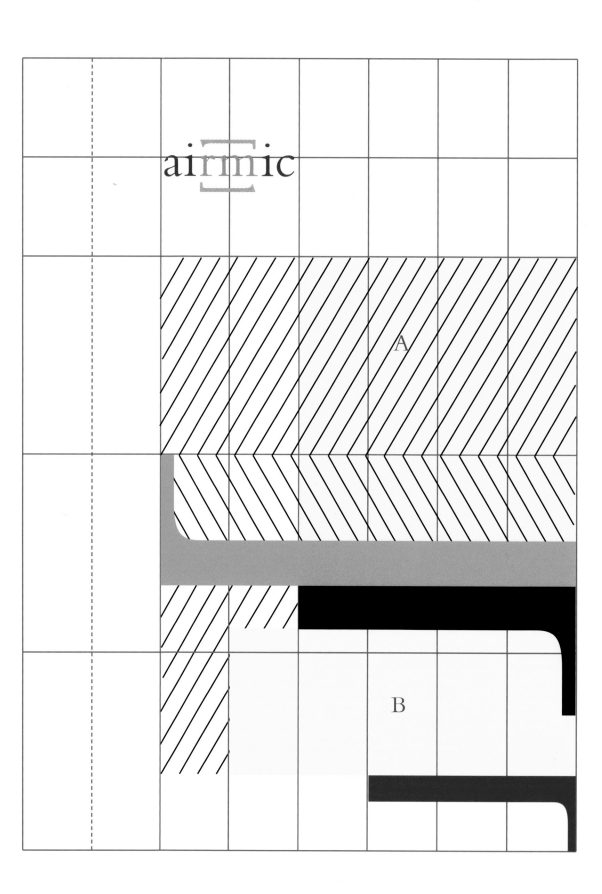

This is an example of a 'balanced formula', leaving discretion and choice to the designer.

AIRMIC achieves its vision for members by:

• Widening the understanding of risk management

• Representing members' views to decision makers

• Playing an active international role

• Providing members with networking opportunities

• Helping members be proactive.

Corporate and individual membership of AIRMIC:

AIRMIC membership provides real benefits to all companies and to those individuals involved in corporate risk management.

Membership details from our London headquarters:

6 Lloyd's Avenue, London EC3N 3AX Tel. 0171 480 7610

Dedicated to raising the profile and standards of risk management

The Association of Insurance and Risk Managers

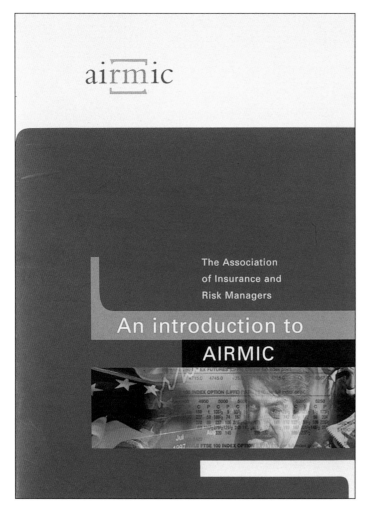

A

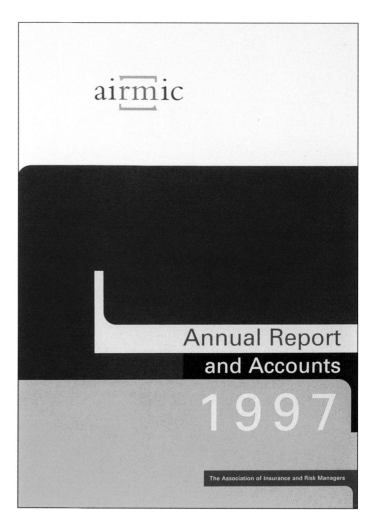

B

A and B are examples where the designer has extended the rules in the style book and yet kept a consistent look and feel – i.e., a consistent visual voice.

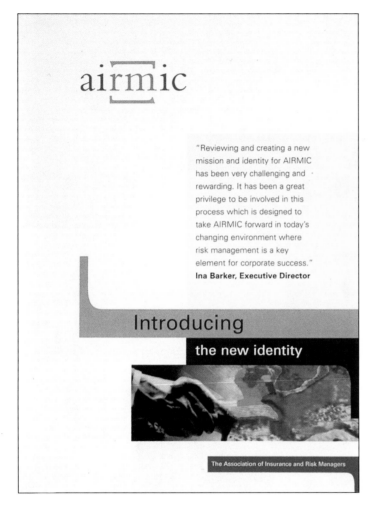

C

D

C and D are examples where the designer has stuck to the rule book and yet the designer of D has managed to produce an inconsistent visual voice by ignoring the visual voice benchmark.

The visual voice benchmark is obviously key to a consistent voice. The next section of this book deals with how to create this benchmark.

British Airways complement their logo on the body of the plane with highly visual and varied tail paintings to underline the proposition that they are 'the world's favourite airline'.

The BBC channel ident shows a hot air balloon floating over British urban and rural landscapes. The visual language is instantly recognisable and distinctive and comes to stand for the BBC, while the logo plays a support role.

Summary so far: Small signs point to a re-contexting of the role of the logo/marque/symbol/fixed masthead, as seen in the examples above and on previous pages.

Yesterday's belief was that as long as the logo appeared in a pre-designated space, at a designated size and colour, surrounded by pre-designed visual elements, then consistency of visual identity would result.

Yesterday the style manual and formula approach reigned supreme. Designers either had very little room for expression or just a small amount. And when the formula is restrictive, the danger was always that the result might be merely conforming but not necessarily consistent.

TODAY, ENLIGHTENED COMPANIES ARE BEGINNING TO COMPLEMENT THE STYLE MANUAL WITH BRAND BOOKS WHICH ADDRESS THE QUESTION OF VISUAL LANGUAGE. A SMALL STEP IN THE RIGHT DIRECTION.

The notion of the monolithic logo has been set aside by CDT Design in favour of a visual language approach to this identity. Variety is the result.P

THE EXAMPLES ON THIS PAGE INDICATE THAT VISUAL IDENTITY IS A BROAD CONCEPT AND THAT A CONSISTENT VISUAL VOICE IS NOT DEPENDENT ON THE USUAL FORMULA APPROACHES. A CLEAR APPRECIATION OF VISUAL LANGUAGE HOLDS THE MASTER KEY.

Consistency of visual voice requires an understanding of visual language.

And an understanding of visual language could result in a freedom for design to flourish, for unique voices to be spoken, for unique layouts to match unique logos, for readers to pick up the key qualities – the brand personality of the organisation – even before they have read a word of text.

THE NEXT STEP IS TO DETERMINE HOW TO GET TO CORE QUALITIES AND THEN HOW TO TRANSLATE THEM INTO A VISUAL VOICE...

Finding the visual voice

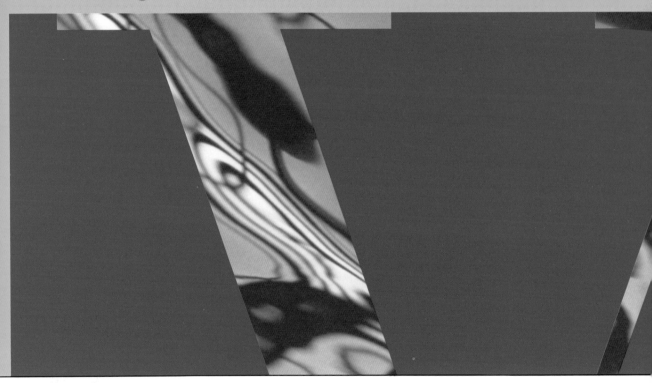

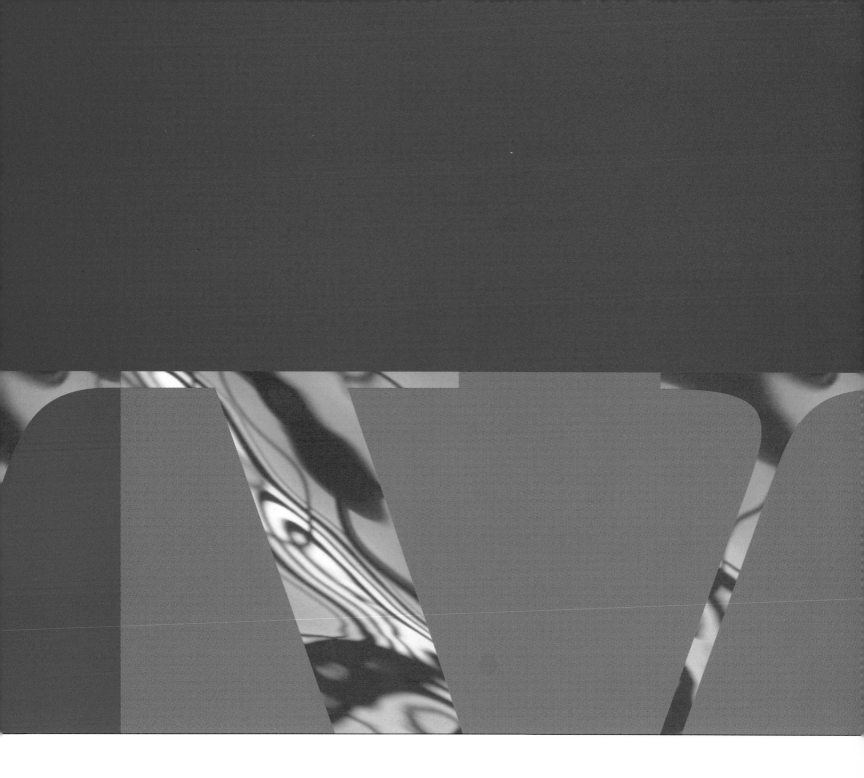

This section looks at simple ways of uncovering the qualities that underpin brand personality and proposes a fresh approach to translating them into the appropriate 'visual voice'.

No one can *create* brand personality.

Every company already has a personality – from global and multinational companies to corner shops. It starts off as as a reflection of the founders' vision or intent and can be spotted in the way the company behaves in the various situations they face. It becomes most visible when the company is under pressure – it's what the management turn to as a point of last resort. At the start of the classic film *Casablanca*, the Humphrey Bogart character is seen to be tough and ruthless, looking after his own self-interest above everything else. But when the chips are down at the end of the film and he has to make a crucial decision, his true character shows itself – noble, principled and selfless. Han Solo goes through the same transformation in the Star Wars trilogy. (Film-makers have known this secret for years!)

Recent research from America shows that companies that have survived and thrived over a long period and through many changes are those that have been guided by a core purpose (why we are really in business) and core values (what we stand for) which never change, and strategic goals – and an envisioned future – that periodically change with market conditions. $1 invested in these visionary companies in 1926 would have grown to around $6,000 by 1990. The same investment in their closest competitors (those founded at the same time, in the same place, offering the same products) would yield just under $1,000. These competitors were characterised as being driven by the bottom line or the usual growth targets that banks and investors like to see – not by vision. The same $1 invested in the general market would have yielded only $450 – 13 times less than the visionaries!

UNCOVERING THE TRUE VISION IS THE FIRST STEP.

INTUITING THE QUALITIES THAT ARE NEEDED TO SUPPORT IT IS THE SECOND STEP.

TRANSLATING THESE ABSTRACT CONCEPTS INTO A TANGIBLE VISUAL LANGUAGE IS THE GOAL OF THIS EXERCISE.

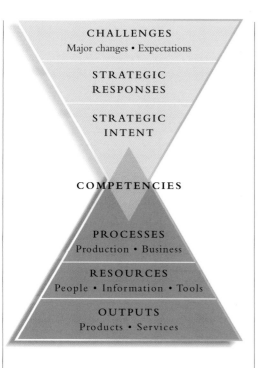

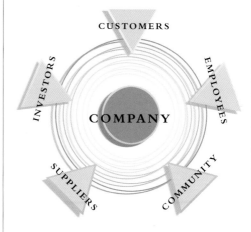

CORPORATE IDENTITY

This is the 'Roman Army' approach – hundreds of hours investigating all facets of the organisation shown in this model. (Even though other models may be used, the same facets are covered):
• What are the challenges – external and internal changes, customer and stakeholder expectations?
• What are the strategic responses required to address them?
• What is the overarching statement of strategic intent that includes all the responses?
• What are the competencies..
• Processes...
• Resources...
• Outputs...
... required to deliver the intent?

The corporate identity approach addresses the way the company is expressed at each level to project an integrated and consistent image.

Visual identity is a small aspect of it.

BRAND PERSONALITY

This is the 'guerrilla team' approach – fast, deep and focused. The target is to get to the values that are implicit in the strategic intent.

All that's required is a list of 3-4 essential, distinguishing and unique qualities that competitors cannot claim.

Words such as: quality, professional, reliable, trustworthy, etc, are likely to be generic to any serious company. They get them to the starting line.

Distinction, on the other hand, may be built around qualities such as *incisive, proactive, cutting edge, passionate, authoritative, flexible, responsive...* in combination.

The overall list of such words might be finite, and a common trap is trying to include them all. But each company with a distinctive personality will have a unique combination of no more than 3-4 qualities that are core to their existence – those that, if abandoned, make a nonsense of what the company is aiming to achieve.

STAKEHOLDER FOCUS

This is the '80:20' approach through which 80% of the key information is obtained with 20% of the effort. It gives a broad direction only, (though in skilled hands it can get to the heart of core values/qualities quite quickly.)

It is based on research which shows that companies who forge positive relationships with the key stakeholder groups experience business success.

The process requires managers to complete a series of sentences as they would ideally like them completed by each of the stakeholder groups.

Example: From the point of view of staff, supply the ideal completion to this sentence (as opposed to what they would actually say): "We enjoy working for the company because..."

Discuss, refine and synthesise the statements till the company's personality starts to emerge. It can be prodded with the question: "In order to be this ideal company, what do you need to <u>feel like</u>? What sort of company can fulfil these expectations?"

ALTERNATIVELY YOU CAN ASK THE STRAIGHT QUESTIONS:
WHY ARE YOU IN BUSINESS? WHAT VALUES DO YOU BELIEVE IN? WHY?

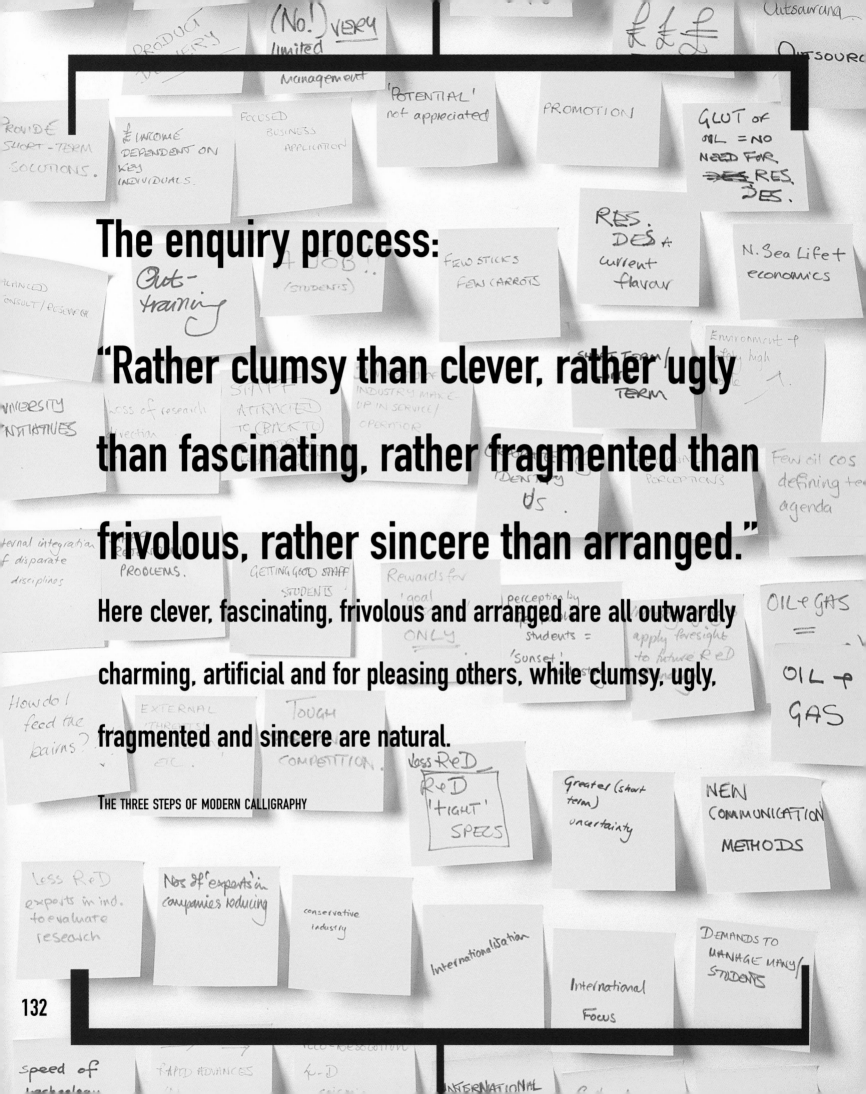

The enquiry process:

"Rather clumsy than clever, rather ugly than fascinating, rather fragmented than frivolous, rather sincere than arranged."

Here clever, fascinating, frivolous and arranged are all outwardly charming, artificial and for pleasing others, while clumsy, ugly, fragmented and sincere are natural.

THE THREE STEPS OF MODERN CALLIGRAPHY

Target: To get to the core qualities that underpin the brand personality – expressed as 3-4 words that convey 'the feel' of the organisation. Why? Because these qualities are most powerfully communicated through the visual language. Ideas, symbols, descriptions are important, but not sufficient on their own. In fact, they can be undermined by an inappropriate visual language.

Context: Whenever a company wishes to communicate through a visual medium, the designer will need to be sure of the 'voice' which best represents the company's position. If the brief does not talk about the 3-4 essential qualities that need to be projected, if the corporate identity manuals do not mention them, then the designer will need to go through a process of enquiry. If a corporate brochure is involved, use the 80:20 rule – get to the bottom fast. If a visual identity is involved, deepen the process... If fundamental assumptions are based on uncertain information, conduct research.

Players: The design team – including the designer. If a designer claims to have no skill or interest in getting an intimate knowledge of the client operation, then what is that designer translating? The equivalent would be a translator of Latin manuscripts saying that they have no knowledge or interest in Latin! This highlights the difference between a designer and a stylist – the stylist is interested in creating vocabulary, the designer in communicating messages through the visual language.

The client team – including all the people who have a role in shaping direction and who are responsible for delivering the vision. A brave client would include representatives from all the five stakeholder groups. Many clients even resist getting non-managerial staff involved – they may be missing a valuable opportunity for testing the gap between the management view and the view of those required to deliver it.

Conditions: Open enquiry, with all pre-conditions, judgements and preferences absent.

True objective: An understanding of the essential beliefs on which the company is based. If financial targets appear to be the over-riding goal, try to get behind them to discover what the company believes it needs to be like in order to deliver them. It might start off as a messy process – clumsy, ugly, fragmented and sincere – but perseverance leads to clarity. Clever, fascinating, frivolous or arranged might lead to a desirable marketing platform, but it may not be true.

Process: Use any of the methods described on the previous pages. Post-it notes are useful to capture raw information and then re-order it into affinity groups. Starting with a huge amount of information, keep reducing and re-reducing it to its essential meaning till you end up with the most distilled essence, expressed in 3-4 words. This is an intuitive process, requiring a nimble and flexible mind that is able to see connections between apparently disparate elements and leap to the essence rather than be stuck on the surface.

The translation process

• Start with the 3-4 words (e.g., Responsive, Forward-looking, Stable – a serious player) written up on a flip chart and ensure that the group re-connects with their qualities.

• Cover a large table with white card and spread out scraps of visual imagery on it — as many as possible (the first 8 leaves of this book begins your collection).

• Ask the client group to remove those that do not EVOKE all the desired qualities together – not one at a time. And put to one side those that particularly evoke the qualities.

> NOTE: You will find that the group starts off in cerebral mode and selects images that illustrate or symbolise the qualities. The facilitator needs to point this out by asking: But does this image make you FEEL responsive, forward-looking, stable? What do these qualities feel like? And does your selection have the same feeling?
>
> **The objective is to side-step the thinking process and get to the feelings. WARNING: Even designers find this hard.**
>
> *The tell-tale sign that the shift from thinking to feeling mode is taking place will be when the disagreements become less. People tend to disagree more about ideas, symbols and illustrations, but tend to agree more about feelings. This shift takes 20-30 minutes.*

• One or two key images will start to emerge as being very close evocations. Use them as a rudder around which to cluster others with a similar feel.

> NOTE: The clue at this stage is to observe what happens when each new image is added or removed. The cluster is 'right' if the eye takes in the whole without moving from image to image.
>
> If the eye keeps being caught by any image, remove it and observe if the remaining ones cohere better. Move image positions to ensure you're not creating a collage.
>
> If an image that does not embody the qualities is added, then the harmony is shattered and the eye picks out individual elements.
>
> If when an image is removed, the whole feels diminished, then that image is probably magnifying some aspect of the qualities.
>
> **By this stage of the process, one is moving from instinct, not thought.**

• Keep refining, be prepared for surprises. When the process is complete, 10–15 images will remain from the 100–200 at the start. 1-2 hours will have passed.

• Step back and confirm: "Are you happy that your company feels like this?"

> *Through this process the client will be educated in the visual language and the basis for the design brief is established.*

Note how the feel of the overall image clarifies and harmonises over the next three pages

Laser Lights Mick Hutson

Start clustering images around the logo below – using the image pieces at the front of this book (plus others you find). Choose the first one that most closely matches the feel of the logo and keep adding others slowly. THE TEST IS THAT THE EYE TAKES IN THE GROUP AS A SINGLE WHOLE – WITHOUT PICKING OUT INDIVIDUAL ELEMENTS.

TRY IT YOURSELF: #2

On a separate board, start with 3-4 new words that have a totally different feel from the ones we have been using (e.g., Caring, Creative and Responsive) and, using the image pieces at the front of this book (plus others you find), create a new benchmark yourself. THE TEST HERE IS TO NOTE IF THE FEEL OF THE TWO BOARDS IS THE SAME.

Start clustering images around the brochure cover below – using the image pieces at the front of this book (plus others you find). Choose the first one that most closely matches the feel of the cover and keep adding others slowly.

THE TEST IS THAT THE EYE TAKES IN THE GROUP AS A SINGLE WHOLE – WITHOUT PICKING OUT INDIVIDUAL ELEMENTS.

If the selection matches, then take the next step and see how closely the inside of this brochure (see page 91- pic 4) benchmarks against the 'visual voice' you have uncovered.

Pros, cons and question marks

THE PROCESS OF CREATING A **VISUAL VOICE BENCHMARK** IS QUITE SUBTLE AND NON-MECHANICAL, MAKING IT NECESSARY TO TEST OUT THE IDEAS IN ACTION RATHER THAN LEAVING THEM AS BOOK THEORY.

Pros

• THE QUALITIES HAVE BEEN ARRIVED AT THROUGH A RATIONAL PROCESS, COMBINED WITH INTUITIVE LEAPS. *Q: How is the intuition involved in the enquiry process?* A: Creating summaries of challenges, responses and the statement of strategic intent is best achieved by taking imaginative leaps – the linkages are not mechanical. Also, during the enquiry stage, sometimes a strange impulse will arise to ask a particular question or to challenge a particular answer – follow it. **The true spirit of open enquiry is creative.**

• THE CLIENT PARTICIPATES AND CREATES THE BENCHMARK. They are educated in the visual language, confirming that everyone reads it and is capable of reading it. From now on, it will be difficult for the client to make choices on the basis of 'like/dislike' or personal taste, because an objective visual voice they have created exists as the benchmark. *Q: How is this followed through?* A: The next section of this book deals with that subject.

• CLEARER BRIEFS CAN BE FORMULATED. In addition to information goals, 'look and feel' benchmarks can also be provided.

• THE RULES OF THE STYLE BOOK ARE COMPLEMENTED WITH AN EMOTIONAL SECTION ON 'LOOK AND FEEL'. In this way conformity is balanced by consistency. *Q: Will this not require designers to be educated to work in a different way with the style book?* A: Yes.

• A LOT OF TIME IS SAVED, ESPECIALLY WHEN CREATING LOGOS. Designers can continue to work from instinct in creating their outputs, but also have a way of ensuring they are on track. *Q: Isn't there a possibility that one can trick oneself into believing that something 'fits', particularly if one likes an image?* A: Yes. It is simply a matter of being rigorous with oneself.

Cons

• THE CLIENT MIGHT NOT WANT TO PARTICIPATE IN CREATING THE BENCHMARK. Then the designers can do it themselves and present the look and feel for client approval. But always get client buy-in.

• THE DESIGNER'S TASTE MIGHT SKEW THE RESULT. Try using very different groups of words to see if the 'look and feel' varies. If not, try again.

Question marks

- ISN'T THIS THE SAME AS A GOOD OLD-FASHIONED MOOD BOARD? Yes in one way, and no in another. The usual type of mood board is sometimes used as a way of stimulating ideas. Solutions arrived at using the usual mood board risk being shaped by images created in the past – true instinct may be hampered. By being abstract, the **visual voice benchmark** by-passes the thinking part of mind and connects directly with the emotions.

- DOESN'T THIS APPROACH LIMIT THE DESIGNER'S ROLE AS INNOVATOR AND CREATOR? One can create hundreds of forms within a mood, just as one can create hundreds of moods with, say, the typeface Helvetica.

- DOESN'T THIS LIMIT THE ROLE OF THE DESIGNER'S INSTINCT? Instinct is a two-edged sword. Sometimes it simply manifests the individual's own personality. Sometimes, something wider flows through the individual. The second is best. To increase the chances of the second, a lot of conscious work needs to take place on the level of skills and experience in the world, because true instinct takes place within the context of what-is. If particular skills are absent then the intuitive solution will not require them. Similarly, if the context is a particular visual voice, then the instinct will accommodate it.

- SURELY THE VISUAL VOICE MUST CHANGE TO SUIT THE VARIOUS AUDIENCE TYPES? In broad terms, the vocabulary might need to change, but what lies behind it – the essence – need not. A confident speaker may change the form of the speech to suit different audiences and yet the essential message and personality of the speaker does not change. That having being said, some major companies do undergo periodic change at a strategic level and will choose to re-visit their visual identity to mark their new position. If they are visionary companies, however, it is unlikely that their core purpose (underpinned by core values) will have changed. It's just the form of expression that changes.

- SURELY THE INFORMATION CONVEYED THROUGH IMAGES AND TEXT IS VERY IMPORTANT? The tone and vocabulary of text can be covered by a visual language that is not consistent with it. The same applies to images. Every image will convey information and evoke emotion at the same time. In some images the information is more dominant and in other the power of evocation rules. Place a powerful image in an indifferent typography and surround it with a wishy-washy colour and note how its power is diminished. *(This topic has been addressed in depth by the author's previous book, 'Designing with Photographs', in Rotovision's Design Fundamentals series.)*

This section looks at how to use the 'visual voice benchmark' in briefing and assessing work.

Instinct takes you most of the way. The conditions required for instinct to take you all of the way are quite demanding – the mind and heart needs to be very steady.

THE HUMAN EYE IS A PRETTY FINE INSTRUMENT. In this experiment, people who happened to be passing were asked:
[1] To adjust the height of the bottom rectangle so that they ended up with the classic Penguin books' proportions.
[2] To fine-tune their final position to what they thought was most pleasing.

In the 'real world' this demanding condition is not the usual starting position. That's when the discipline of the rational can be brought in as a useful support for the freedom of instinct.

THE PENGUIN GRID (SEE PAGE 110) IS SUPERIMPOSED ON THEIR ANSWERS. It can be seen how close some have got. In a couple of instances, very small adjustments are required to be spot-on. Intuition is powerful and the rational, conscious template can be used to make fine adjustments.

The visual voice benchmark can be used in the following situations:

1. When creating logos.

2. When briefing designers of corporate/marketing literature, etc.

3. When designing corporate/marketing literature, etc.

4. When assessing various design proposals.

It becomes a useful diagnostic tool for both designers and commissioners of design. It helps designers fine-tune their creations and helps commissioners assess work more or less objectively. Judgements of commercial work can rise above the 'like/don't like' polarity and can address the more fundamental question of appropriateness and consistency of image.

There is one important caveat: just because the final answer projects a consistent voice, the solution might not necessarily be the best!

The inside cover flap of this book is a detachable visual benchmark that applies to work in this book.

Cut it out and perform the series of test described in the next pages.

The underpinning qualities are:
- Responsive
- Forward-looking
- Stable
– a serious player

[This book has focused on pure visual language and has not touched on the idea, symbol or information conveyed through it – a vast subject on its own. If content is weak or ideas non-existent, then the solution will be weakened.

1. The logo test...

Test it first in black and white to avoid an undue skewing of choice because of colour harmony.

Assume that the designer has been very prolific and created all these marques in response to the brief. On their own, each has its strengths, so how is the final choice made?

• Photocopy this page and cut out the individual marques. Place them one at a time onto the visual benchmark. Which one 'fits'? (Refer back to page 134 for a description of the process.)

• This benchmark was used in creating the logo on page 138. How well does it fit?

2. The layout test...

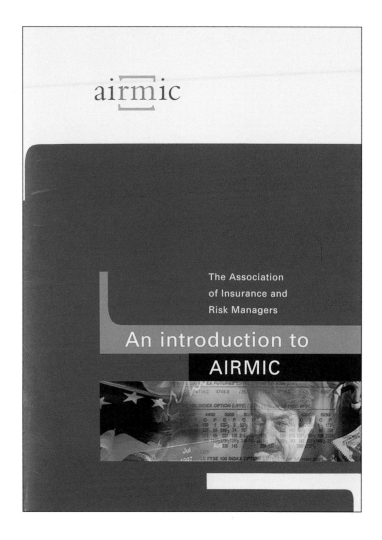

The above cover has been created to fit with the benchmark. Does it?

• Test each of the Airmic materials against the benchmark (pages 123-125). It should demonstrate that, of all the items, cover D on page 125 is a bad fit. Here the formula has been followed, but the voice is inconsistent.

• Test each of the covers on pages 93-97 against the benchmark. If they come close to a fit, then some of the qualities being projected are shared.

3. The imagery test...

The appropriateness of photographs or illustrations can also be benchmarked... Try these.

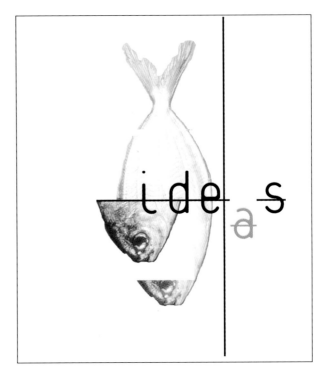

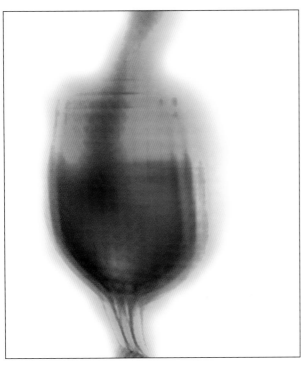

Imagery cannot be considered in abstract. Cropping, sizing, proportion, surrounding it with colour and type, etc., might well change the impact. Pages 30-33 show how dramatic these influences can be. Page 154 shows subject and style in harmony.

[Section 4 of Rotovision's 'Designing with Photographs' systematically explores the effect of each element of visual language on an image.]

4. Typography and grid

There are literally thousands of permutations possible. Here are just two to test against the benchmark…

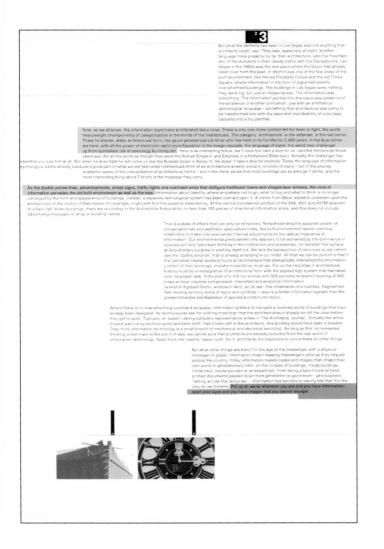

5. Briefing

In addition to spelling out the key marketing points...

and in addition to supplying any corporate visual guidelines...

... supply a visual benchmark to the designer and ask them to ensure the work matches the feel.

If no corporate visual guidelines exist, there are two short-term possibilities...

1] Work with the design team to create a benchmark by clustering imagery around the logo.

2] Work with the internal management team to determine the core qualities that underpin the corporate positioning. Then work with the design team to create a benchmark.

The long term requires a clear policy on brand personality to be developed and communicated internally to all those in the organisation who are responsible for commissioning design. This is a lengthy process and can meet with deeply entrenched views and cultural barriers. So, it must be approached with the expectation that the journey will take time.

6. Assessing

There are two levels at which the submissions can be tested:

1] Are the ideas consistent with the qualities and are they illustrated as such?

2] Is the visual language consistent with the benchmark?

A judgement will need to be made between which of the two design routes has the most potential for delivering an integrated solution. Sometimes, ideas-led designers might not have a sufficient visual literacy, and some style-led designers cannot generate winning ideas.

The ultimate aim is integration right across the medium of communication — from idea, to imagery, to voice — verbal and visual.

This journey has come to its end.

The chosen route has gone deep instead of broad, and so much more could be said. It has be less concerned with the surface form of design than with its deeper, hidden emotive messages.

The field of visual language is wide. No person on the planet is unaffected by it. But who really knows what effect daily exposure to walls of billboards and flyposters has on the mind of society? What is red really doing? Or the sweeping curve of the Helvetica 'a'?

Three persuasive channels are well known: you can hypnotise a person (put their mind to sleep), brainwash them (disorientate the mind) or reason with them (wake the mind up).

Visual language is called upon to create these effects. Design can put you into a cosy nostalgic dream, rattle the brain with its pyrotechnics or open the heart.

It's too important to be left to chance and accident.

When we start from principle, identity design isn't really complex. Every living entity has an identity – it's what essentially defines it. That's the simple starting point.

It may be possible to cover the true identity, but it is difficult to continue acting from a false identity for too long. (Madonna may be a 'virgin' or a 'whore', the 'girl next door' or a 'vamp' at different stages of her career; but there are few who believe that Madonna is any of these deep down.) True identity is what inheres – working invisibly to shape the ways of doing things, processes of thought, the feel of the environment and the rest.

Visual identity design, then, simply involves *uncovering the true identity* and then manifesting it through the visual language – an act of translation and evocation. So, whether creating the identities for an individual consultant, a suite of brochures, or packaging, or a business unit with in a larger organisation or the large organisation itself, we go through the same basic process of analysis and translation.

The first step involves uncovering what they believe they are – deep down. By asking pressing questions about present and future challenges, by adding to these the present and future expectations from customers, staff, society at large – and challenging any off-the-top-of-the-management-theory-shelf answers – we start to get a glimpse what the enterprise really believes it is. Its values become apparent.

This brings us to the second step – making these intangible values tangible.

Here, too, we return to principle: all communication takes place through language, but not all languages involve words. Body language, the language of sound, visual language are commonly recognised. Each has its equivalent of syntax, grammar, punctuation; each has the power to evoke an emotional response. The task of creating a visual identity requires the manipulation of type, colour, image, texture, space to communicate – i.e., evoke – the values that underpin the identity.

This journey has explored one unique method of working *with clients* to arrive at a collection of images that evoke a desired response – a visual benchmark. Any item of design can be placed among these images and evaluated by the extent to which it harmonises, or not, with them. If it doesn't, then the design is likely to be evoking qualities that conflict with the overall mood of the collection.

Then comes the third step: the actual design process itself. Who really knows how it takes place? Designers absorb a lot of information and then start making marks on paper. Too much information tends to block the process. The wrong sort of information side-tracks the outcome. The greater the exposure the designer has to myth, art, literature, etc., the richer is the mix available for the symbolic level of the design.

In the end, marks are evaluated and they are either liked or disliked – we need to make sure, however, that the response is as objective as possible. This is where evaluating the design against the visual benchmark is the key.

The question no longer is: "Do I like it or not?"; it becomes: "Is it communicating the right things about us or not?" That's how identity becomes real.

Peter Bonnici
London, 1998

Acknowledgements

A number of the ideas in this book have been developed over a long period of time and refined through hours of talking with other designers, photographers, illustrators and artists. Of these, one needs special mention. Jon Henry has been a collaborator, friend and fellow searcher on the journey of understanding. Together we wrote a tiny book in 1989 with the intentention of de-mystifying the design process for clients. Some of the insights from that book are still valid. He has been a foil for ideas in this book and remains a passionate proponent of the visual language approach. Thanks also to Barbara Mercer at Rotovision for seeing that the potential of our earlier book together, *Designing with Photographs*, could be extended. (And also for indulging my poor approach to even extended, extended deadlines). Hélène, Pippa, Martin and Melanie at Quadrant have read and commented on the ideas, and helped with artwork and designs. Special thanks are also due to Charlie Milligan who has provided many of the images used in this book – some from his own portfolio and a number specially shot. Finally there are all those designers whose work makes one reel with amazement and whose skills and approach keep raising the standards and opening up new visual territory.

Credits

PHOTOGRAPHY

P18: Flowers, from *Abstracts*, copyright-free images by Michael Banks.

P19: Top, Flowers, Annabel Baker, +44 (0)181 318 2972 (m) 0385 292992

P19: Bottom, Flowers, Hannah McPherson (m) 0976 677 084

P26: Couple, Charlie Milligan +44 (0)181 676 0349 (m) 0831 391 175

P31: (left to right)
• Charlie Milligan (as above)
• James Hunkin +44 (0)171 794 8463

P32: (From *Designing with Photographs*)
• Landscape, Clive Boursnell +44 (0)171 722 1998 (m) 0831 647 244
• Abstract, Barbara and Zafer Baran +44 (0)181 948 3050

P33: (From *Designing with Photographs*)
Faces (Top row, l to r),
• Sebastaio Salgado/Network +44 (0)171 831 3633
• David Scheinmann +44 (0)171 439 3231
• Jillian Edelstein/Network +44 (0)171 831 3633

Bottom row (l to r)
• (Personal collection)
• James Hunkin (as above)
• David Scheinmann (as above)

P144-145
Zac Macaulay/Ethos Represents +44 (0)171 735 7006

TYPOGRAPHY

P156:
(l) Octavo 88.6
(r) RayGun, *David Carson*

BACKGROUND READING

The Transformation Imperative, Achieving Market Dominance through Radical Change by THOMAS E. VOLLMANN *(Harvard Business School Press)*. The elements of the diagnostic model illustrated on page 131 are explained and developed in detail in this book. It calls for explicit links to be made across every facet of an organisation so that change is integrated, consistent and desirable.

Built to Last, Successful Habits of Visionary Companies by JAMES COLLINS & JERRY PORRAS *(Century Business Books)*. The essential role of vision – core purpose, core values, stretching goals and a visualised future – in building companies with sustainable greatness.

Living Tomorrow's Company by MARK GOYDER *(Gower Publishing Limited)*. The approaches of successful companies which are build on strong stakeholder relationships instead of just financial goals.

The Three Steps of Modern Calligraphy by GU GAN *(Chinese Book Publishing House)*. Inspiring lessons on the three steps from skills to intuition. Its principles apply to any creative endeavour.

Designing with Photographs, by PETER BONNICI & LINDA PROUD *(RotoVision)*. An exploration of the hidden power of photography and how it can be supported or under-mined by visual language.